NATURAL RESOURCES

Animals

NATURAL RESOURCES

ANIMALS

CREATURES THAT ROAM THE PLANET

Julie Kerr Casper, Ph.D.

CHELSEA HOUSE
PUBLISHERS

An imprint of Infobase Publishing

Animals

Chelsea House
An imprint of Infobase Publishing
132 West 31st Street
New York NY 10001

ISBN-10: 0-8160-6353-2
ISBN-13: 978-0-8160-6353-6

Library of Congress Cataloging-in-Publication Data

Casper, Julie Kerr.
    Animals : creatures that roam the planet / Julie Kerr Casper.
        p.   cm.—(Natural resources)
    Includes bibliographical references and index.
    ISBN 0-8160-6353-2 (hardcover)
    1. Zoology—Juvenile literature. I. Title. II. Series.
    QL49.C376 2007
    590—dc22   200603022

Chelsea House books are available at special discounts when purchased in bulk quantities for businesses, associations, institutions, or sales promotions. Please call our Special Sales Department in New York at (212) 967-8800 or (800) 322-8755.

You can find Chelsea House on the World Wide Web at http://www.chelseahouse.com

Text design by Erik Lindstrom
Cover design by Ben Peterson

Printed in the United States of America

Bang NMSG 10 9 8 7 6 5 4 3 2 1

CONTENTS

PREFACE
NATURAL RESOURCES:
PRICELESS GIFTS FROM THE EARTH

Mankind did not weave the web of life.
We are but one strand in it. Whatever we
do to the web, we do to ourselves . . .
All things are bound together.

—Chief Seattle

The Earth has been blessed with an abundant supply of natural resources. Natural resources are those elements that exist on the planet for the use and benefit of all living things. Scientists commonly divide them down into distinct groups for the purposes of studying them. These groups include agricultural resources, plants, animals, energy sources, landscapes, forests, minerals, and water and atmospheric resources.

One thing we humans have learned is that many of the important resources we have come to depend on are not renewable. *Nonrenewable* means that once a resource is depleted, it is gone forever. The fossil fuel that gasoline is produced from is an example of a nonrenewable resource. There is only a finite supply, and once it is used up, that is the end of it.

While living things such as animals are typically considered renewable resources, meaning they can potentially be replenished, animals hunted to extinction become nonrenewable resources. As we know from past evidence, the extinctions of the dinosaurs, the woolly mammoth, and the saber-toothed tiger were complete. Sometimes, extinctions like this may be caused by natural factors, such as climate change, drought, or flood, but many extinctions are caused by the activities of humans.

Overhunting caused the extinction of the passenger pigeon, which was once plentiful throughout North America. The bald eagle was hunted to the brink of extinction before it became a protected species, and African elephants are currently threatened with extinction because they are still being hunted for their ivory tusks. Overhunting is only one potential threat, though. Humans are also responsible for habitat loss. When humans change land use and convert an animal's habitat to a city, this destroys the animal's living space and food sources and promotes its endangerment.

Plants can also be endangered or become extinct. An important issue facing us today is the destruction of the Earth's tropical rain forests. Scientists believe there may be medicinal value in many plant species that have not been discovered yet. Therefore, destroying a plant species could be destroying a medical benefit for the future.

Because of human impact and influence all around the Earth, it is important to understand our natural resources, protect them, use them wisely, and plan for future generations. The environment—land, soil, water, plants, minerals, and animals—is a marvelously complex and dynamic system that often changes in ways too subtle to perceive. Today, we have enlarged our vision of the landscape with which we interact. Farmers manage larger units of land, which makes their job more complex. People travel greater distances more frequently. Even when they stay at home, they experience and affect a larger share of the world through electronic communications and economic activities—and natural resources have made these advancements possible.

The pace of change in our society has accelerated as well. New technologies are always being developed. Many people no longer spend all their time focused in one place or using things in traditional ways. People now move from one place to another and are constantly developing and using new and different resources.

A sustainable society requires a sustainable environment. Because of this, we must think of natural resources in new ways. Today, more than ever, we must dedicate our efforts to conserve the land. We still live in a beautiful, largely natural world, but that world is quickly changing. World population growth and our desire to live comfortably are exerting pressures on our soil, air, water, and other natural resources. As we destroy and fragment natural habitats, we continue to push nonhuman life into ever-smaller pockets. Today, we run the risk of those places becoming isolated islands on a domesticated landscape.

In order to be responsible caretakers of the planet, it is important to realize that we humans have a partnership with the Earth and the other life that shares the planet with us. This series presents a refreshing and informative way to view the Earth's natural resources. *Agriculture: The Food We Grow and Animals We Raise* looks at agricultural resources to see how responsible conservation, such as caring for the soil, will give us continued food to feed growing populations. *Plants: Life From the Earth* examines the multitude of plants that exist and the role they play in biodiversity. The use of plants in medicines and in other products that people use every day is also covered.

In *Animals: Creatures That Roam the Planet,* the series focuses on the diverse species of animals that live on the planet, including the important roles they have played in the advancement of civilization. This book in the series also looks at habitat destruction, exotic species, animals that are considered in danger of extinction, and how people can help to keep the environment intact.

Next, in *Energy: Powering the Past, Present, and Future,* the series explores the Earth's energy resources—such as renewable power from water, ocean energy, solar energy, wind energy, and biofuels; and non-renewable sources from oil shale, tar sands, and fossil fuels. In addition, the future of energy and high-tech inventions on the horizon are also explored.

In *Lands: Taming the Wilds,* the series addresses the land and how civilizations have been able to tame deserts, mountains, arctic regions, forests, wetlands, and floodplains. The effects that our actions can have on the landscape for years to come are also explored. In *Forests: More Than Just Trees,* the series examines the Earth's forested areas and how unique and important these areas are to medicine, construction, recreation, and commercial products. The effects of deforestation, pest outbreaks, and wildfires—and how these can impact people for generations to come—are also addressed.

In *Minerals: Gifts From the Earth*, the bounty of minerals in the Earth and the discoveries scientists have made about them are examined. Moreover, this book in the series gives an overview of the critical part minerals play in many common activities and how they affect our lives every day.

Finally, in *Water and Atmosphere: The Lifeblood of Natural Systems*, the series looks at water and atmospheric resources to find out just how these resources are the lifeblood of the natural system—from drinking water, food production, and nutrient storage to recreational values. Drought, sea-level rise, soil management, coastal development, the effects of air and water pollution, and deep-sea exploration and what it holds for the future are also explored.

The reader will learn the wisdom of recycling, reducing, and reusing our natural resources, as well as discover many simple things that can be done to protect the environment. Practical approaches such as not leaving the water running while brushing your teeth, turning the lights off when leaving a room, using reusable cloth bags to transport groceries, building a backyard wildlife refuge, planting a tree, forming a carpool, or starting a local neighborhood recycling program are all explored.

Everybody is somebody's neighbor, and shared responsibility is the key to a healthy environment. The cheapest—and most effective—conservation comes from working with nature. This series presents things that people can do for the environment now and the important role we all can play for the future. As a wise Native-American saying goes, "We do not inherit the Earth from our ancestors—we borrow it from our children."

ACKNOWLEDGMENTS

While we interact with many animal species every day, many people are not aware of just how much we depend on animal life. Animals play a critical role in everyone's existence. They provide us with useful products, contribute to medical advancements, provide valuable services, give us opportunities to enjoy nature, entertain us, and act as faithful companions.

I hope to instill in you—the reader—an understanding and appreciation of animal life and its role in our environment. Perhaps raising awareness of animals and all they do and have to offer will spur the desire to conserve this precious resource in order to avoid the endangerment and extinction of species.

I would sincerely like to thank several of the federal government agencies that study, manage, protect, and preserve animal life—in particular, the U.S. Fish and Wildlife Service (FWS), the Natural Resources Conservation Service (NRCS), the National Park Service (NPS), the U.S. Forest Service (USFS), and the Bureau of Land Management (BLM) for providing an abundance of resources for information on this important subject. I would also like to acknowledge and thank the many universities across the country and their biology departments, as well as private organizations that diligently strive to protect our precious animal resources.

INTRODUCTION

Over millions of years, animals have adapted to various environments on Earth. Animals exist everywhere—from the steamy rain forest jungles to the polar ice caps; from the highest mountains to the deepest oceans. Animal life is crucial. Animals provide critical links in the food chain as well as in the biogeochemical cycles that help keep the Earth's environment healthy.

Although animals have evolved over geologic time in response to the Earth's constantly changing environments and while the extinctions of certain species are normal, during no other time in the Earth's history has the extinction rate climbed as high as it has today. The reason is simple: human interference. Because of expanding populations and conversion of the land to urbanization, agriculture, and other human-based uses, wildlife habitat is being gobbled up at a rapid rate. As habitat critical to an animal's survival is lost, eventually so is the animal itself. Scientists believe that there is a vast amount of animal life on Earth yet to be discovered, but if humans do not make conservation of wildlife habitat a priority, we may never know what life existed and its potential importance to humans.

This volume in the Natural Resources series focuses on the many aspects that make animals such a vital resource. Chapter 1 looks at the biosphere, the role of biodiversity, why animals exist where they do, and how animals have adapted and survived through eons of change on the planet.

Chapter 2 looks at the fossil record of ancient species and what important information this gives scientists. It also looks at rates of extinction and what the true costs are.

Chapter 3 examines energy flow through the ecosystem, food webs, and the delicate balance of biogeochemical cycles.

Chapter 4 addresses development of the land and its effects, the necessity of responsible land management, and how high-tech computer tools are helping land managers achieve their goals.

Chapter 5 discusses the many uses of animals and how they affect our lives every day, from products to research, their roles at home and at work, in nature, in education, in entertainment, and recreation. It also focuses on how we protect and provide for animals—for their well-being and welfare.

Chapter 6 looks at the importance of animals and all of the goods and services they provide to humans and the ways in which they have greatly improved the quality of our lives.

Chapter 7 addresses the management of the land, water, animals, and environment as parts of a working system and how each component must be present to have a healthy environment. It examines the causes of endangerment, the truth about poaching, the effects of environmental disasters, and laws that protect endangered species.

Chapter 8 presents the successful methods of the conservation, planning, and restoration needed to keep wildlife flourishing.

Finally, Chapter 9 looks at the future of animals and the actions each of us can take to ensure not only their survival, but a healthy and solid future for them so that they will be there for future generations to enjoy.

WILDLIFE CONCEPTS AND GEOGRAPHICAL DISTRIBUTION

Animals live everywhere on Earth—in every type of climate, on every type of terrain. About two million **species** have been named. Scientists believe there still may be 50 million more to be discovered. In order to understand the impact that humans have on **biodiversity**, it is necessary to know how many species there are, information about these species, and how the numbers are changing. This chapter focuses on the biosphere and richness of animal species on Earth, the role of biodiversity, the existing **biomes** and **habitats**, animal adaptations and mechanisms of **survival**, animal diversity, and the future of species.

THE BIOSPHERE

The biosphere is the organization of life. Scientists have recognized that life can be organized into several different levels of function and complexity. These functional levels include species, **populations**, communities, and **ecosystems**.

Species

Species are the different kinds of organisms found on Earth, initially defined in terms of their appearance. Members of a species look similar to other members of the species. In addition, members of a species should be able to interbreed, be physiologically similar, and occupy similar habitats.

Scientists use **taxonomy** to name and classify organisms. This is useful because assumptions can be made about organisms based on what category they belong to. Likewise, once something is known about a member of a group, inferences can be made about the group as a whole. The table below lists types of organisms, how many have been classified, and how many are estimated still to be discovered.

Organisms Known and Yet to Be Discovered

Organism	Number classified	Number of potential species yet to be discovered
Viruses	5,000	500,000
Bacteria	4,000	400,000–300 million
Fungi	70,000	1 million–1.5 million
Protozoa	40,000	100,000–200,000
Roundworms	15,000	500,000–1 million
Mollusks	70,000	200,000
Crustaceans	40,000	150,000
Spiders and mites	75,000	750,000–10 million
Insects	950,000	8 million–100 million
Vertebrates	45,000	50,000

(Source: From the PBS program NOVA, www.pbs.org.)

Scientists classify organisms into seven hierarchical levels of taxa. They range from most inclusive to the least inclusive, as follows:

Kingdom	Most inclusive, largest group
Phylum	
Class	
Order	
Family	
Genus	
Species	Least inclusive, smallest group

To illustrate, a human being is classified as follows:

Kingdom	Animalia
Phylum	Chordata
Class	Mammalia
Order	Primates
Family	Hominidae
Genus	Homo
Species	sapiens

The scientific name of an organism is composed of the genus and species. For example, in the example of humans, the scientific name is *Homo sapiens.*

Population

A population comprises all the individuals of a given species in a specific area or region at a certain time. Animal populations do contain genetic variation within themselves and between other populations. For example, basic genetic characteristics such as hair color, eye color, or size may differ slightly from individual to individual. In addition, not all members of the population are equal in their ability to **survive** and reproduce so the species continues.

Community

A **community** refers to all the populations in a specific area or region at a certain time and involves many interactions among species. They may interact in their acquisition of food or other environmental resources.

Ecologists believe that a community that has high diversity is more complex and stable than one that has low diversity. They have found that the food webs of communities with high diversity are more interconnected. Greater interconnectivity makes these systems better able to deal with disturbance. For instance, if a species is removed, those species that relied on it for food can turn to other species that occupy a similar role in the ecosystem.

Ecosystems

Ecosystems (short for "ecological systems") vary in size. They can be as small as a pond or as large as the Earth itself. Any group of living and nonliving things interacting with each other can be considered an ecosystem. They are units that result from the interactions of **abiotic**, **biotic**, and cultural components. Because they are systems, they are a combination of interacting parts. All ecosystems are referred to as "open systems" because energy and matter are transferred in and out of them. The largest ecosystem people can relate to is the Earth, because it constantly converts solar energy into many different kinds of organic products.

Natural ecosystems are made up of abiotic factors (air, water, rocks, and energy) and biotic factors (plants, animals, and microorganisms). The Earth's biosphere, including the atmosphere (air), hydrosphere (water), and lithosphere (land), is a working system of living things and their physical and chemical environments.

Changes in any component of ecosystems (such as temperature, nutrient availability, and population density) will result in dynamic changes to the nature of these systems. An example of this is a forest fire. A fire changes the ecosystem because it removes large trees, destroys the shrubs and mosses that covered the forest floor, and destroys the nutrients that had been stored in all the biomass (living matter, such as

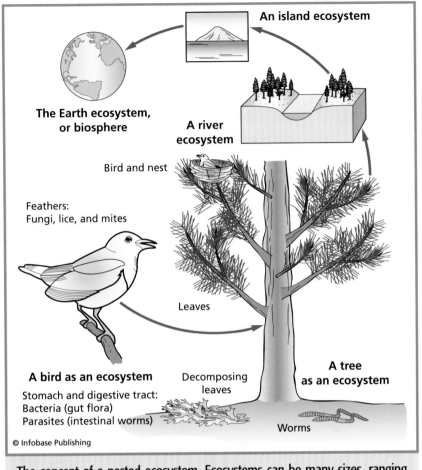

An island ecosystem

The Earth ecosystem, or biosphere

A river ecosystem

Bird and nest

Feathers: Fungi, lice, and mites

Leaves

A tree as an ecosystem

A bird as an ecosystem

Decomposing leaves

Stomach and digestive tract: Bacteria (gut flora) Parasites (intestinal worms)

Worms

© Infobase Publishing

The concept of a nested ecosystem. Ecosystems can be many sizes, ranging from a broad area of land to a single bird.

vegetation). Once the area recovers from the burn, the community that was once mature trees is now a community of grasses.

THE ROLE OF BIODIVERSITY

Biodiversity is the term used to describe the variety of life on Earth. It encompasses all the animals, plants, and microorganisms that exist on the planet, the genetic variety within these species, and the variety of ecosystems they inhabit. Biodiversity can exist at three levels:

- Species diversity—this is the variety of species of animals, plants, and microorganisms on Earth or in a given area capable of reproducing fertile offspring.
- Genetic diversity—this is the variety of genetic characteristics found within a species and among different species. An example of **genetic diversity** in humans is the variation in hair and eye color, height, and facial appearance.
- Ecosystem diversity—this is the variety of natural systems found in a region, a continent, or on the planet. A mountain, a prairie, and a wetland are examples of three different types of ecosystems.

Within each ecosystem there are habitats that may also vary in size. A habitat is a place where a population lives in a community of living things that interact with the nonliving world around it to form an ecosystem. Most animals are only adapted to live in one or two habitats. For example, a bear can be seen in a temperate forest or alpine area, but not in a wetland or desert. Likewise, saltwater fish—such as the shark—could not live in the arctic or a freshwater lake. Some animals **migrate** in the spring and migrate again in the fall in search of warmer habitats with an abundance of food, such as humpback whales and many species of birds.

The habitat must supply the needs of the organisms, such as food, water, appropriate temperature, oxygen, and minerals. If a population's needs are not met, it will move to a better habitat. Two different populations cannot occupy the same **niche** at the same time, however, because they would be competing against each other for survival. Because of this, the processes of **competition**, predation, **cooperation**, and **symbiosis** occur.

A habitat is the place where many species live naturally. Billions of different things live together in a habitat. Some beings are so tiny, they can only be seen with a microscope. Others, like whales, horses, or giraffes, are huge. All species play a significant role in making the habitat a healthy place to live. Several populations can share a habitat and can coexist with each other. For example, in a coral reef, many fish coexist. Likewise, in a rain forest, a multitude of populations not only coexist, but distinct populations coexist in multiple levels of the rain forest. For example, in the higher canopies, several species of parrots may occupy the habitat.

Biodiversity is important in a habitat for several reasons. The different populations fill specific positions in the **food chain**. If a component in the food chain—plant or animal—disappears, it upsets the ecological balance of the habitat and can ultimately destroy it.

The Earth's biodiversity has been in a constant state of change for as long as life has existed. Periodic natural events, such as meteor impacts, volcanoes, glaciers, climate change, drought, fire, and flooding have disturbed ecosystems and led to the reduction or extinction of species, reducing biodiversity. As civilization has developed, humans have had an important impact. Several human activities directly or indirectly threaten biodiversity.

For example, humans often disturb natural ecosystems. Because each ecosystem consists of a community of animals, plants, soil, minerals, water, and air, each component of the system fills a special role. It is a delicate balance, and humans have the ability to destroy this natural balance. When the balance is disrupted, this can trigger a multitude of other disruptions because all the components are tied together, thereby threatening the health and existence of the entire ecosystem.

Humans have an adverse impact when they pollute the environment. Human activity can pollute the water, air, or soil and harm biodiversity. When humans introduce nonnative species of plants and animals (plants and animals that don't normally live in a particular habitat), it also disrupts biodiversity and may have a negative impact because it causes competition with native species for survival.

Destruction of habitat is another way humans can adversely affect biodiversity. When natural lands—such as deserts, wetlands, or grasslands—are converted to urban areas or farms, it leads to the loss of natural plant and animal habitats.

Overexploitation is another problem. When humans hunt animals or use animals for food, raw materials for industry, or for their fur, it can threaten the continuation of species and even lead to extinction.

Biodiversity is very important. Everything that lives in an ecosystem is part of the web of life—including humans. Maintaining a wide diversity of species in each ecosystem is necessary to preserve the web of life that connects and supports all living things.

The more biodiversity there is—both within species and between species—the greater chance of that habitat surviving. Even if some species are destroyed, chances are good that others will survive when biodiversity is high. That is why **biologists** often measure the health of a habitat based on its biodiversity.

BIOMES OF THE EARTH

Descriptions of the environment, such as temperature and rainfall, are used to group habitats together. Habitats of similar climate and vegetation are called biomes. In different parts of the world, the same biome may contain different species, but similar life-forms can always be identified. For example, a pine tree is a dominant form in a temperate forest regardless of where the temperate forest is located. The Earth's biomes can be classified in several ways, including the following:

- Desert
- Scrubland
- Tundra
- Boreal forest (taiga)
- Temperate grassland
- Temperate forest
- Savanna
- Tropical rain forest
- Mountain
- Aquatic

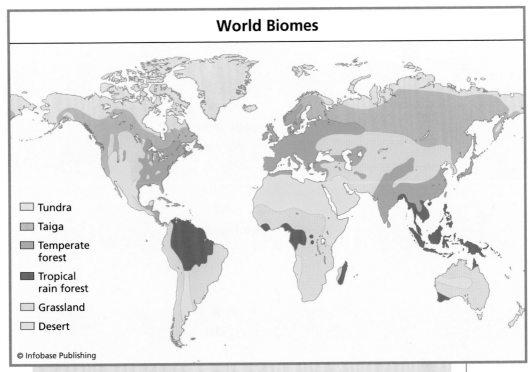

World Biomes

☐ Tundra
◫ Taiga
◫ Temperate
   forest
◼ Tropical
   rain forest
☐ Grassland
☐ Desert

© Infobase Publishing

Major biomes of the Earth.

Biomes are extremely important. They have changed and moved many times during the history of life on Earth. More recently, human activities have drastically altered these communities.

Desert

Deserts cover more than one-third of the world's land. They are some of the hottest, driest places on Earth. Temperatures can be as high as 120°F (50°C). Deserts can also be cold. Some deserts can drop to temperatures of −4°F (−20°C). The little rain that falls evaporates quickly. Even though the conditions are harsh, deserts provide a home to many animals. Some desert animals cope with the sun's heat by burrowing beneath the sand, because sand stays cooler than the desert surface. Some **mammals**—such as the naked mole rat—hardly ever leave

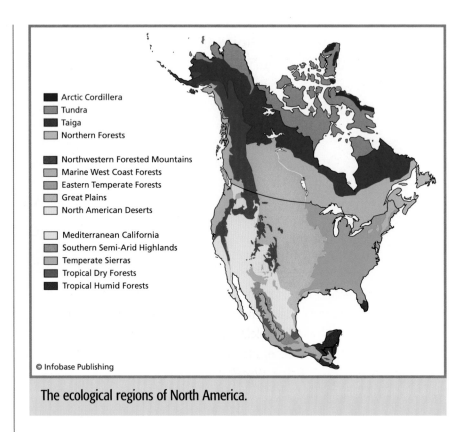

The ecological regions of North America.

Legend:
- Arctic Cordillera
- Tundra
- Taiga
- Northern Forests

- Northwestern Forested Mountains
- Marine West Coast Forests
- Eastern Temperate Forests
- Great Plains
- North American Deserts

- Mediterranean California
- Southern Semi-Arid Highlands
- Temperate Sierras
- Tropical Dry Forests
- Tropical Humid Forests

© Infobase Publishing

their burrows. Some animals avoid the scorching sun by only coming out at dawn and dusk, such as the North American kangaroo rat, the American ground squirrel, and the North African jerboa.

Scrubland

Scrublands are places with hot summers and cool, moist winters. Because of the hot, dry summers, trees don't grow very tall. Animals in these regions must be able to adapt to many different conditions because they are generally located near oceans.

Tundra and Polar

These regions—located at the far northern and southern latitudes—are characterized by long, dark winters. Because they are located at the

Examples of ecosystems: (a) Mountain; (b) Island. The ecosystem determines which animals can survive in that environment, such as the caribou that lives in the Arctic regions. Different wildlife, such as parrots, live in coastal and tropical areas. If an animal cannot adapt to the environment, it will not survive. *(a, courtesy of the U.S. Fish & Wildlife Service, Dean Biggins; b, Nature's Images, Julie A. Kerr)*

Earth's poles, the sun never rises far above the horizon. Beyond the ice-covered Arctic, however, is the tundra, which supports a fairly large amount of animal life. Each summer, the vegetation that appears during the short growing season attracts many birds and other animals.

Boreal Forest

The boreal forest—also called the *taiga*—is an extremely large biome covering 6,800 miles (4,506 kilometers) across the northern hemisphere. It also exists high on mountain ranges such as the Rocky Mountains and Appalachians in the United States and the Alps in Europe.

The boreal forest is characterized by a cold climate, scarce rainfall, and a short growing season. When boreal forests are located in the interior portions of continents, the temperatures can get colder than the polar regions further north. Interior continental locations are colder because they do not have the benefit of nearby warmer ocean air to modify the climate. Frost covers the areas most of the year, which causes much of the ground to be permanently covered in water because the frost keeps the water from being able to drain away. The severity of winter limits the diversity of animal life. Not only are physical conditions harsh, but there often is little food.

Due to the harsh conditions, many of the animals do not live in the boreal forest the entire year. Birds only migrate into the area during the summer, moving south to a warmer climate for the rest of the year. Animals that do live there year-round have adapted to life in this harsh climate.

Insects, such as mosquitoes, gnats, and midges, are abundant during spring and summer, serving as food for migratory birds.

Temperate Grassland

The grasslands of Asia are called *steppes*, those of South America are called *pampas* and *campos*, and those of North America are called *prairies*. Many animals live in these areas. Different animals are found in different parts of the grasslands based on the annual rainfall of the area.

The North American prairie is divided into three categories: (1) short grass, where grass stays below 20 inches (51 centimeters) tall; (2) mixed grass, where grass ranges from 20 to 60 inches (51–152 cm) tall; and (3) eastern tall grass, where grass can grow as high as 10 feet (3 meters).

The Asian steppe is divided into an eastern and western range. The eastern steppe is higher and drier. It can also be divided into western forest steppe (this area contains pine, oak, and birch trees), open steppe (where trees are scarce), and southern semidesert (where desert vegetation grows).

The various landforms—such as marshes, streams, rocky slopes, and rock outcrops—provide niches for different kinds of animals. Muskrats and water snakes are found in water bodies such as creeks and rivers; frogs, crickets, and water bugs are found in the shallow tide

Wildlife of the World's Biomes

Biome	Representative Animals	
Desert	Mammals	Desert kit fox, wild horses, kangaroo rat
	Birds	California quail, golden eagle, gila woodpecker
	Invertebrates	Scorpion, tarantula, ant, trap-door spider, black widow spider
	Reptiles	Gecko, lizard, snake, gila monster
Scrubland	Mammals	Jackrabbit, roe deer, sheep, goat, kangaroo, wolf, cougar
	Birds	Imperial eagle, vulture
	Insects	Dung beetle, swallowtail butterfly
Tundra and Polar	Mammals	Polar bear, whale, seal, musk ox, lemming, arctic fox, wolf, snowshoe hare, caribou
	Birds	Arctic tern, falcon, eagle, penguin, snowy owl
	Insects	Beetle, spider, blowfly, mosquito
Boreal Forest	Birds	Goshawk, nuthatch
	Herbivores	Deer, beaver, vole
	Predators	Lynx, weasel, gray owl, wolverine, wolf
	Insects	Gnat, mosquito, midge
Temperate Grassland	Birds	Canada goose, wild turkey, white pelican
	Herbivores	Pronghorn sheep, prairie chicken
	Predators	Coyote, eagle, bobcat/lynx, gray wolf
	Insects	Water bug, cricket, dung beetle
Temperate Forest	Herbivores	Red deer, roe deer, fallow deer
	Amphibians	Frog, newt, salamander
	Birds	Sparrow hawk, woodcock, chaffinch
	Insects	Butterfly, deadwood beetle
Savanna	Grazers	Giraffe, impala, elephant, wildebeest, zebra, kangaroo, wallaby
	Predators	Wild dog, cheetah, leopard, lion
	Scavengers	Hyena, vulture
	Insects	Locust, termite, leafhopper
Tropical Rain forest	Mammals	Elephant, deer, gorilla, jaguar, leopard
	Birds	Hornbill, toucan, harpy eagle, fruit pigeon
	Other	Tree frog, sugar glider, green python
Mountain	Predators	Mountain fox, mountain lion (puma), snow leopard
	Mammals	Llama, alpaca, mountain sheep
	Birds	Andean condor, eagle, falcon, snow finch, ptarmigan

(Source: Oracle Education Foundation)

pools. The biome is also home to animals that graze (such as cattle and llamas), burrowing animals, and many different kinds of insects.

Temperate Forest

Temperate forests used to cover large areas of eastern North America, Europe, and Asia. Human activity, however, has eliminated much of these forested areas. Today, only isolated regions of the forests can be found in the Northern Hemisphere. Fortunately, many of these forests are professionally managed and protected.

The tree habitats support many animals. The forests of North America have five times as many species of trees in them as the forests in Europe. These forests provide a home for many rare and endangered animals. Animals that live in the forest clearings include birds and insects, such as the speckled wood butterfly.

Savanna

Savanna is a Spanish word that means "treeless plain." Savannas are located between the Tropic of Cancer and the Tropic of Capricorn—the region of Earth extending from 23.5° North to 23.5° South latitude of the equator. They are large expanses of grass with only scattered trees. Another characteristic of a savanna is low rainfall (although not as low as a desert). Massive **herds** of grazing animals—along with **predators** such as lions, leopards, and cheetahs—inhabit the savanna.

Temperatures are high because savannas are located in the tropical latitudes. Most of the rain falls during two time periods during the year. Savannas support a large amount of biodiversity.

Tropical Rain Forest

The tropical rain forest is the richest and most diverse biome in the world because of the warm, damp climate. A total of more than 1.5 million species of plants and animals live in the world's rain forests.

Animals that live in the highest trees almost never visit the ground. These include insect-eating birds, like the hornbill and toucan. The main canopy of the forest traps moisture and shields the rain forest from the wind. This is the zone where the majority of animal species are found—scientists have discovered 600 different species of beetles in one canopy.

Big cats—such as the jaguar and leopard—live under the shady canopy, waiting to catch their **prey**. The forest floor is home to deer, gorillas, and elephants.

Mountain

One thing that distinguishes mountains from other ecological systems is that each mountain can have its own distinct climate and collection of plants and animals. Some mountains are permanently capped with snow. Mountains are usually wetter than lower lying areas. Whether the side of the mountain faces the sun also has an impact on the vegetation that grows there, which also helps determine which animals will live there. One side of the mountain can be warm and damp, the other cold and windy.

A few animals can survive in the harsh conditions of the mountains. Larger animals are usually agile, such as the mountain goat, and many animals adapt survival mechanisms to live in this environment.

The highest altitude a vertebrate—a bird—has ever been seen is at the top of Mount Everest. Only the strongest birds—such as the eagle, falcon, and condor—can withstand the harsh wind. These birds feed on smaller birds. The smaller birds feed on the seeds and insects.

Aquatic

Water makes up the largest biosphere—oceans cover 75% of the Earth's surface. Characteristics such as light, temperature, pressure, and nutrients all affect the variety and abundance of animal life in aquatic habitats. In general, the number of species is greatest in the equatorial regions and least near the poles.

The transparency of the water allows light to travel through. Phytoplankton, and many other organisms, use light to make food through the process of photosynthesis. The surface waters, rich in nutrients, provide 12.6 million tons a year to fisheries.

The ocean regions are separated into zones: intertidal, pelagic, benthic, and abyssal. All four zones have a great diversity of species. The intertidal zone is where the ocean meets the land and where the waves and tides come in and out. This zone supports small snails, crabs, sea stars, worms, clams, and small fish.

The pelagic zone includes water farther from land and in open ocean. This zone provides a home for many species of fish and mammals, such as whales and dolphins. The benthic zone is the area below the pelagic zone, but does not include the deepest zone. Animals in this zone include bacteria, fungi, sponges, sea anemones, worms, sea stars, and fishes.

The deep ocean is the abyssal zone. The water in this region is extremely cold (−16°F or 3°C), highly pressured, high in oxygen content, but low in nutritional content. It supports many **invertebrates** and fish. Hydrothermal vents, sometimes called black smokers, host huge populations of bacteria because of the large amounts of hydrogen sulfide and other minerals they emit, providing the basis of the food chain in the abyssal zone.

Coral reefs are highly diverse ecosystems that exist in warm, shallow waters. These areas provide habitat for corals, microorganisms, invertebrates, fish, sea urchins, octopuses, eels, and sea stars.

Estuaries are areas where freshwater streams or rivers merge with the ocean and provide a home for worms, oysters, crabs, and waterfowl. Freshwater regions—such as ponds, lakes, streams, rivers, and wetlands—have a low salt concentration (usually less than 1%). The animals in these regions have adjusted to the low salt content and would not be able to survive in areas of higher salt concentration, such as the ocean. The shore region of a lake is the littoral zone. It is the warmest layer because it is shallow and can absorb more of the sun's heat. Animals found in this zone include snails, clams, insects, crustaceans, fish, and amphibians. These animals are food for other animals such as turtles, snakes, and ducks.

The limnetic zone—the open water of a lake—provides a home for a variety of freshwater fish. The deepest zone of the lake—the profundal zone—is dark, cold, and dense. Animal life in this zone is composed of heterotrophs, which eat dead organisms and use oxygen for cellular respiration.

Wetlands have the highest species diversity of all ecosystems. Many species of amphibians, reptiles, birds (such as ducks), and furbearers can be found in wetlands. Some wetlands have a higher salt content and provide habitat for shrimp and shellfish.

ANIMAL ADAPTATIONS—MECHANISMS FOR SURVIVAL

Populations depend on their environment or habitat to meet the basic needs for survival. For an animal to survive in a habitat, oftentimes it must make adaptations in order to survive. These adaptations can be physical changes over time or behavioral changes.

To survive the lack of water, desert animals have developed other adaptations. For example, the kangaroo rat saves water by eating its own droppings. Some lizards soak up water from the damp sand through special scales. Camels conserve water in reserves by adjusting their body temperature. Other animals, such as tortoises, are able to withdraw enough water from their food to satisfy their needs.

Because the tundra is so cold, its animals have had to adapt in order to survive. Because the climate is often cold and windy, most animals have developed compact bodies with short limbs, bills, and wings to conserve heat. Other animals have thick deposits of **blubber** (fat) or dense layers of feathers or fur to insulate them. Polar bears have two layers of fur. Many animals burrow into the ground, as it also serves as a good insulator against harsh climates. Some animals burrow into the snow in order to avoid the strong winds typical in the polar regions.

Animals—like penguins—cluster in large groups of several thousand to keep each other warm. In Antarctica, some animals have developed a special protein compound that allows them to be able to withstand extreme temperatures.

In the African grasslands, speed is an important adaptation for animal survival. Because there are few trees or places for animals to hide, speed is important for both predators that are hunting and the animals that are fleeing them.

A polar bear is an example of an animal that has had to adapt to survive in its environment. Its two layers of fur are an adaptation that helps protect the animal from sub-zero Arctic temperatures. *(Courtesy of the U.S. Fish & Wildlife Service, Scott Schliebe)*

In a tropical rain forest, monkeys use their arms, legs, and tails to swing from branch to branch. Parrots have specialized feet with two curling front toes and two curling back toes to help them hang on to branches. Snakes—such as boa constrictors—spend their days curled around branches or vines; and on the forest floor, jaguars' spots help them to be better hunters by making them hard to see among the speckled shadows of the rain forest floor.

In the boreal forests (taiga), animals have adapted to the cold climate. Since there is not much heat from the sun to warm their eggs, taiga reptiles give birth to live young. Many of the animals are large, which makes it easier for them to conserve heat. Because of this, elk and wolverine are common in the taiga. In order to capture prey, the wolverine's well-furred feet enable it to run across the thin crust of snow.

In mountain environments, small mammals live in burrows and **hibernate** during the winter. Larger animals are usually very agile. Animals must overcome several things to live in high altitudes. One is the lack of oxygen. Usually, animals gradually adapt to the environment by increasing their heart rate, rate of respiration, and the number of oxygen-transporting cells in their blood. Another adaptation is the ability to reduce heat loss. Fur and other insulation help with this.

ANIMAL DIVERSITY

All animals are members of the Kingdom Animalia, also called Metazoa. The animal kingdom can be broken down into specific categories—amphibians, arthropods, birds, bony fishes, echinoderms, insects, mammals, mollusks, reptiles, and sharks.

Amphibians are animals that live part of their lives in water and part on land. There are about 5,500 known species of amphibians, divided into three main groups: (1) salamanders, newts, and mudpuppies; (2) caecilians; and (3) frogs and toads.

Amphibians cannot regulate their own body heat, so they depend on warmth from sunlight to become warm and active. They also cannot cool down on their own, so if they get too hot, they have to find a burrow or other area with shade.

Young amphibians do not look like their parents. As they grow, they change in body shape, diet, and lifestyle, through a process called **metamorphosis**. An example of this is a tadpole that turns into a frog as it ages.

Arthropods include an incredibly diverse group of taxa such as insects, crustaceans, spiders, scorpions, and centipedes. There are more species of arthropods than species in all the other phyla combined. (A phylum—plural is phyla—is a ranking category in biological taxonomy that represents the largest generally accepted grouping of animals and other living things with certain evolutionary traits.) Many arthropods have been responsible for the most devastating plagues and famines humans have known. Other species of arthropods are essential for our existence, directly or indirectly, by providing humans with food, clothing, medicines, and protection from harmful organisms.

Birds are **vertebrates**, with a backbone and skeleton, although some of the bones are hollow to keep the bird light. Their forelimbs have the same bones as the human arm, but they are highly modified to form the structure for wings. There are more than 8,800 known species of birds. Bony fish also comprise a large group of vertebrates. Fish are of enormous economic importance to humans. People consume fish through fishing and aquaculture, making them an essential form of protein for millions of people around the world.

Echinoderms, such as sea urchins and sea stars, play an important role in their ecosystems. Research on echinoderms has helped scientists learn more about animal fertilization and development. Many echinoderms are easy to culture and use in science labs, and they produce a large number of eggs. Sea urchins are edible and often served in sushi bars.

There are about one million named species—and many times more that are not named—in the insect class. Insects can be found in almost all terrestrial and freshwater habitats, from the driest deserts to freshwater ponds and from the tropical rain forest to the cold arctic.

Insects range in shape and form, but all insects share certain features: They have a body composed of relatively large compound eyes, antennae, two pairs of wings, and three pairs of walking legs. Insects are extremely valuable to humans—without them, we could not exist. They are a fundamental part of the ecosystem. Insects are important for pollinating plants; decomposing organic materials; helping recycle carbon, nitrogen, and other nutrients; producing food (such as honey); and manufacturing useful products such as silk.

All mammals share three characteristics not found in any other type of animals: They have three middle ear bones, they have hair, and they produce milk by modified sweat glands called mammary glands. Mammals can be found in all continents and seas and consist of about 5,000 species.

There are many endangered species, such as the gray wolf shown here. It is important to understand that endangered means there is still time to save the species, but it takes a well thought out, dedicated recovery plan to make it successful. *(Courtesy of the U.S. Fish and Wildlife Service, Gary Kramer)*

Reptiles include turtles, snakes, lizards, and crocodiles. Reptiles have scales composed of protein, lungs instead of gills for breathing, and 3- or 4-chambered hearts.

THE FUTURE OF SPECIES

Wildlife cannot exist without its habitat, but saving the habitat does not ensure the survival of wildlife. Key animals may be threatened and lost as a result of natural forces, management choices, or other human activities, such as overhunting and recreation.

Many species over the years have become threatened, or **endangered,** and some have become **extinct**. *Endangered* means that a species is facing a high risk of becoming extinct in the wild.

Some animals have become extinct in recent years. For example, in the early 1800s, millions of passenger pigeons existed. They were overhunted until, in 1914, the last passenger pigeon on Earth died. Also, in the 1800s, the quagga—a zebralike animal—was hunted to extinction in southern Africa. In the late 1600s, the last dodo birds vanished from their island home of Mauritius in the Indian Ocean.

Today, many animals face extinction. Many animals that were once very common are now rare and face extinction if action is not taken to save them. Endangered species today include giant pandas, tigers, gorillas, bald eagles, elephants, and orangutans. Animals become threatened if they lose their natural habitat—rain forests are being cut down, swamps drained, and grasslands being converted into cities—because they suddenly have nowhere to go.

Poachers also threaten animals' futures. For example, jaguars, tigers, and leopards are hunted for their fur; elephants are killed so people can make jewelry out of ivory tusks; and rhinoceroses are killed for their **horns**. In Chapters 7 and 8, this book will explore habitat preservation and important animal protection issues.

EVOLUTION, ADAPTATION, AND EXTINCTION THROUGH TIME

Life on Earth has changed dramatically over time. Animals have had to adapt to a variety of conditions, such as major geologic events, climate changes, changes in ecosystems and environment, changes in continental positions, and major extinctions. This chapter explores the science of **paleontology** and how the study of fossils enables scientists to understand how animal life has adapted. It examines extinctions throughout history and explains different theories scientists have about them. It then outlines animal distributions over time and reasons why some species exist only in specific places. Finally, this chapter addresses recent extinctions and the role humans have played in them.

LEARNING FROM THE FOSSIL RECORD

Many scientists, such as **paleontologists** (scientists that study life from past geological periods), **geologists** (scientists who study the history, formation, and processes of the Earth), and biologists (scientists who study plant and animal life and their associated processes), use the fossil record to learn about the past history of the Earth. Learning about the past helps scientists have a better understanding of the geologic processes that continue today, past and present biodiversity, species origination and extinction, past and present climates, ocean processes, and atmospheric changes. Scientists have been able to reconstruct the Earth's history over the past 3.5 billion years based on the discovered fossil record. (The Earth is 4.6 billion years old, and fossils have been traced back 3.5 billion years.)

Paleontology is the study of the development of life during the history of the Earth. To understand animal life, it is also necessary to understand **geology** and processes that have shaped the Earth. When scientists study the distribution of organisms today and relate them to the environmental variables that control those distributions, they can use this present-day knowledge to reconstruct past environments by using fossilized remains that resemble modern organisms as paleoenvironmental indicators. A **paleoenvironment** is an environment that existed on the Earth in ancient times. Scientists study fossils, along with **biostratigraphy** (layers of rock of different ages with fossils embedded in them), to reconstruct these past environments. It is through this type of knowledge that scientists can locate deposits of oil and gas—oil and gas formed from dinosaur remains and the paleoenvironment during that geologic time period. By studying the fossils (for presence of dinosaurs) and stratigraphy (the rock formations that could hold oil and gas), geologists are able to explore for this important energy resource.

Just as it is possible to look at the present as a starting point to discover the past, it is also possible to study the past in order to understand the present and predict the future. If scientists can understand how organisms in the past responded to environmental changes, then they can use that information to predict how future natural or human-influenced environmental change might affect the life on Earth.

Fossils are remains or traces of ancient living things. Fossilization is not a common event—it requires specific environmental conditions for a fossil to form. In addition, not all parts of animals become fossilized. It may not be possible to know all the details of what an ancient animal (or plant) looked like because many parts of the anatomy may not become fossils.

The chances of a given individual being preserved in the fossil record are very small, although some organisms have a better chance than others because of the composition of their skeletons or where they live. Animals with bones are made up of different parts that can separate after death. In addition, the different parts can be transported by currents to different locations and be preserved separately, making it difficult to interpret the fossil record.

Much of the potential information is lost in the fossilization process because, most of the time, only the bones and teeth are preserved. Once paleontologists can reconstruct an animal based on the fossil record, they can make an analysis of the animal based on the fossil remains. It is often possible to deduce more about the animal, its capabilities, and habitat based on sound biological principles. Things like **social** behavior, vocalization, and hair or skin color are more of a guess.

By looking at the fossil remains, scientists can get a good idea of what the environment was like that the animal thrived in. Scientists know that organisms must be adapted to their environment in order to survive. They look at these special adaptations for clues as to the animal's behavior and habitat. For example, a stegosaurus skeleton indicates it had only one toe bone on each foot. It did, however, have specialized adaptations on its back and tail. It had huge armor plates and tail spikes, indicating that it was not a fast runner but had specialized adaptations for defense against predators.

When paleontologists study fossilized teeth, the teeth can also relay critical information. If the teeth are flat (like a horse's), they were probably used for grazing, which means the animal was an herbivore and lived in an environment with an abundance of specific vegetation. This, in turn, tells scientists about what the climate was like.

If an environment changes and the animal cannot adapt to the new conditions, it will not survive. This basic rule helps scientists piece together past climates.

Change in environments is an important topic. It is often easy to take the world's present environments for granted and assume they've always been the way they are now. Environments have, however, changed in the past, and they are always in the process of changing. Environmental change is not easy to understand because it often takes place so slowly that direct observation is difficult. The fossil record, on the other hand, contains a compressed view of many millions of years during which environments changed just as they do today. Like time-lapse photography, changes in the fossil record are much more obvious and easier to see.

Fossils can indicate climate changes, which are related to food supply because plants are very sensitive to climate. If an herbivore's favorite food disappears, the herbivore cannot survive. If the herbivore does not survive, the carnivores that eat the herbivore cannot survive. As explored in the next chapter, these changes can have a far-reaching effect on the food webs that support a habitat.

The relationship between human activities and environmental change and extinction is critical for scientists to understand, as well as the importance of maintaining the diversity of life. This is because each component is not independent of the system—the system works as a whole, with each component playing a significant role.

Dating Techniques

There are three basic dating techniques used by scientists to determine the age of animals that once lived on Earth: (1) radiometric dating, (2) stratigraphy, and (3) molecular clocks.

Geologists use radiometric dating to estimate how long ago rocks formed and to infer the ages of fossils contained within those rocks. The universe is full of naturally occurring radioactive elements. Because radioactive elements decay, this means they are unstable. Over time, an unstable radioactive "parent atom" will decay into a stable "daughter atom." For example, uranium 238 decays into bismuth 214 at a known rate.

When igneous rocks are formed from volcanoes, the radioactive atoms are trapped inside and then begin to decay at a predictable rate. By measuring the quantity of unstable parent atoms left in a rock and comparing it to the number of stable daughter atoms there are—because the decay rate is predictable and can be measured—scientists can estimate the amount of time that has passed since the rock was formed.

Fossils are usually found in **sedimentary rock**—not igneous rock. For rocks that are younger than fifty thousand years old, sedimentary rocks can be dated using radioactive carbon. In order to date older fossils, however, scientists look at the rock strata—the rock formations above and below the sedimentary rock the fossil is stuck in—for layers of igneous rock. Scientists can date the igneous rock using the slower-decaying elements—such as uranium and potassium—typically found in it. By determining the ages of rock layers above and below the bed containing the fossil, scientists can determine the oldest and youngest age range the fossil lies within. This is called "bracketing" the age of the fossil. For example, they could say a fossil is between 100,000 and 150,000 years old.

When using stratigraphy as a dating method, fossils can be dated relative to one another by identifying their positions in layers of rock—layers of rock are known as *strata*. Fossils found in lower, deeper-buried layers were deposited earlier and are older than fossils found in the layers above. This is referred to as the law of superposition.

This process is fairly straightforward in areas that have horizontally bedded layers of rock. It gets more complicated, however, when geologic forces—such as earthquakes and volcanoes—rearrange the layers. When this occurs, a mass of rock may cut across other strata, or the natural erosion process may have disrupted the regular pattern. Rock can also be melted, bent, twisted, and turned upside down from the powerful forces inside the Earth. When this happens, the oldest rocks are those that were cut through by other rocks. The next oldest rocks are those that did the cutting through the older rocks, and the youngest

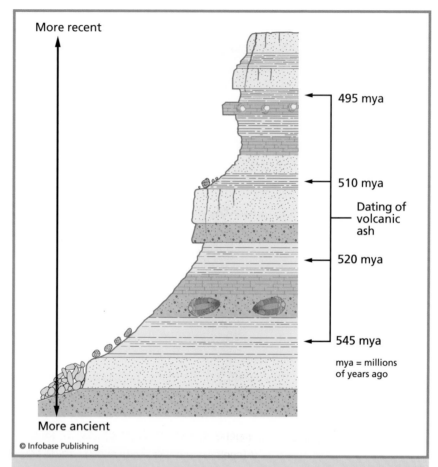

More recent

495 mya

510 mya

Dating of volcanic ash

520 mya

545 mya

mya = millions of years ago

More ancient

© Infobase Publishing

Fossils are generally found buried in layers of rock and sediment. By dating the layers in which the fossil is found (or the layers above and below the specimen), scientists can estimate the fossil's age. This technique is known as stratigraphy.

rocks are those that lie in layers above these other rocks and have not been disturbed. By studying the stratigraphy, scientists can get a good idea how old the rock—and also the fossils—are.

Dating by molecular clock is based on changes in genetic makeup. Evolutionary biologists have been investigating the possibility that some evolutionary changes occur at a regular, predictable rate over

A dinosaur skeleton provides evidence of past life. By reconstructing skeletal remains, paleontologists can fit together pieces of the past and gain a better understanding of what types of animal life existed on Earth. The exhibit above is at the University of Utah Museum of Natural History. *(Nature's Images)*

time. Over the course of millions of years, mutations can occur in a strand of DNA at a reliable rate. When biologists can identify specific characteristics in DNA, it becomes a powerful tool for estimating the dates when genetic lineages split and one species became two distinct species. When calculating an age using these "molecular clocks," scientists also use the relative dating and absolute dating techniques discussed previously. In putting together the history of life, scientists look for patterns that exist, based on the concept that species have common ancestors. By looking at so-called family trees, scientists can determine biological classifications of life.

By correlating fossils from different parts of the world, scientists are able to assign relative ages to rock formations and fossils. By using this information from areas around the world and correlating the studies, scientists have been able to establish the geologic time scale. This relative time scale divides the vast amount of Earth history into basic sections based on geological events, such as mountain building; sea-level changes; and depositional events, such as volcanic eruptions and glaciations. It is also based on major biological events, such as the appearance of certain life-forms, their abundance and distribution, and their extinction, as shown in the table on page 31.

EVOLUTION, ADAPTATION, AND EXTINCTION

Extinction is the end of a species, a family, or a larger group of organisms. Evolution, adaptation, and extinction are natural occurrences in the history of life on Earth. Extinctions have been occurring constantly, usually matched by the rate at which new species appear. As life evolves and adapts, biodiversity increases.

There have, however, been periods in the Earth's history when biodiversity crashes and much of the life disappears. When more than 50% of the Earth's species vanish in a short geological time period of a few million years, this is called a **mass extinction**.

Some scientists have suggested that there is a cycle of mass extinction with a major die off at a predictable interval. Most agree on six major extinctions during geologic time: (1) Late Cambrian, (2) Late Ordovician, (3) Late Devonian, (4) End Permian, (5) Late Triassic, and (6) End Cretaceous.

Some form of climatic change has probably been involved in all of the mass extinctions, even if the change itself was the result of another factor—like a volcano or an asteroid. Glaciations—global cooling and the formation of huge sheets of ice—are the most important type of change attributed to mass extinctions.

Adaptation of Life Throughout Time

Years ago	Event
130,000	Modern humans evolve. Their descendents create cave paintings.
4 million	In Africa, "Lucy," an early hominid, lives. The ice ages begin, and many large mammals go extinct.
20 million	Grass begins to grow.
35 million	Camels appear.
65 million	A huge asteroid hits the Yucatan Peninsula and ammonites and nonavian dinosaurs go extinct. Birds and mammals are among the survivors.
100 million	Ants appear.
120–130 million	Earliest flowers evolve, and dinosaurs dominate the landscape.
225 million	Dinosaurs and mammals evolve. Pangaea, the supercontinent, begins to break apart.
248 million	Over 70% of the land life and 90% of the ocean life go extinct during the Earth's largest mass extinction. Ammonites survive.
250 million	The supercontinent called Pangaea forms. Conifer-like forests, reptiles, and ancestors of mammals are common.
300 million	Earthworms appear.
350 million	Ferns appear.
360 million	Four-limbed vertebrates exist, and seed plants and large forests appear.
400 million	Sharks appear.
420 million	Land plants evolve, drastically changing Earth's landscape, and new habitats are created.
450 million	Arthropods live on land. Their descendants evolve into scorpions, spiders, mites, and millipedes.
500 million	Vertebrates evolve. Invertebrates are common in the oceans.
555 million	Multicellular marine organisms are common.
600 million	Jellyfish appear.
1 billion	Green algae form.
3.5 billion	Unicellular life evolves. Photosynthetic bacteria begin to release oxygen into the atmosphere.
3.8 billion	Replicating molecules form (what DNA evolved from).
4.6 billion	The Earth forms.

Climate change causes extinction by changing the type and availability of ecological niches. If species are forced to either adapt or migrate to another location and cannot, they become extinct.

Scientists have proposed several theories to explain the cause of mass extinction: asteroids, volcanoes, climate change, sea-level change, and some other unusual theories. It is difficult for scientists to agree on just one theory because the actual cause could have been a combination of more than just one cause.

A giant asteroid colliding with the Earth at the end of the Cretaceous—the extinction that marked the end of the dinosaurs—was proposed by physicist Luis Alvarez in 1980. He proposed that based on an unusually large amount of a rare element called iridium found in the rocks between the Cretaceous and Tertiary periods. Iridium is extremely rare in the Earth's crust, but is much more common in asteroids. If a large enough asteroid slammed into the Earth, it could have sent a huge shock wave around the globe—similar to a nuclear explosion—and the immense heat and winds would have caused widespread fires of global proportions. Earthquakes and huge tidal waves would have been significant; a cloud of vaporized water would have filled the atmosphere; and the cloud of debris could have caused global cooling, darkness, and acid rain. There is evidence of an asteroid impact at the end of the Cretaceous—it is called the Chicxulub Crater.

Other scientists think mass extinctions could have been caused by volcanic activity. The end of the Cretaceous is associated with large-scale volcanic activity. Immense clouds of gas and debris could have had deadly effects on the animals and plants. Some scientists believe volcanoes could have been responsible for the high amounts of iridium found in the Earth's crust during the Cretaceous.

Changes in sea level are often suggested as a cause of mass extinction. When sea levels change, habitats are disrupted or destroyed. Sea-level change is also connected to the formation of ice sheets and periods of glaciations. For example, as the ice sheets take up seawater, the oceans shrink; then when the ice melts, the sea level rises again. Changes in sea level can have other effects, as well. Changes in the

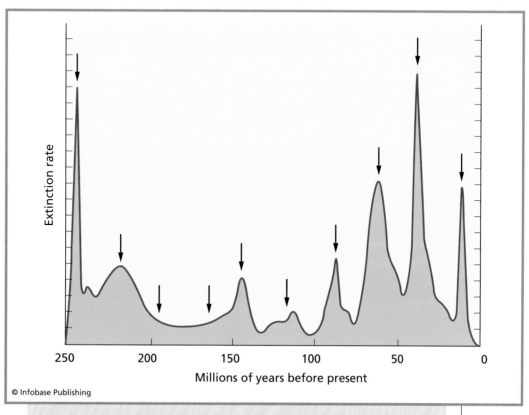

Extinction rate (y-axis)

Millions of years before present (x-axis): 250, 200, 150, 100, 50, 0

© Infobase Publishing

Evidence exists that mass extinctions (indicated by black arrows in the graph above) occur at regular time intervals of approximately 26 million years.

oxygen distribution or salinity in the oceans have been associated with changes in sea level and could have a large enough impact on marine environments to cause mass extinctions. In fact, scientists have linked periods of sea-level change to most of the mass extinctions.

Other, less popular theories for mass extinction have been proposed; for example, cosmic radiation from nearby exploding stars—supernova—that may have caused radiation poisoning and cancer, leading to mass extinction; nickel poisoning spreading across the Earth in a cloud from an asteroid impact; or egg-eating mammals that ate the dinosaur eggs have all been proposed.

As research is carried out on mass extinctions of life, scientists' knowledge of the fossil record has advanced, reaffirming the theory of a cyclical mass extinction—every 26 million years or so. Alfred Fischer and Michael Arthur first suggested this concept. Research was further expanded by researchers using data collected by David Raup and John Sepkoski, who constructed graphs of mass extinctions of marine (ocean) families through time. As seen in the graph on page 33, the peaks coincide with most major events of extinction throughout the Earth's history.

Biodiversity is higher now than it has ever been before. There are more species living on Earth today than at any other time in the Earth's history. But even with the millions of species alive on the Earth today, it represents only a tiny fraction of the number of species that have ever existed—some scientists believe that over time there have been up to five billion species. This illustrates the huge role extinction has played in the Earth's history—more than 99% of the species that have ever existed have become extinct.

Unfortunately, humans play a big part in destroying the diversity of environments on Earth today. Through slash-and-burn agricultural

The Disappearance of the Dodo

The dodo is the most famous extinct species. This unique, flightless bird only existed on the Mauritius—a small island in the Indian Ocean. Because these birds had no natural enemies and food was abundant on the ground, they were **tame** and had no reason to fly, so their wings had become useless. Then, in 1507, Portuguese sailors discovered the island. The sailors and settlers began eating the dodos and then later introduced pigs and monkeys to the island. The dodo had no effective defense mechanisms to keep the pigs and monkeys from eating their eggs and hatchlings. At the same time, settlers began cultivating more and more of the island's fertile land, effectively destroying the dodo's habitat. By 1680, the dodo had become extinct.

practices in the rain forest and urbanization in the developed world, thousands of species are being driven to extinction—from microorganisms and small insects to large mammals. Humans may be the driving force in modern mass extinction, because species are being lost at a rate that is several hundred times more than the "natural" extinction rate.

ANIMAL DISTRIBUTIONS AROUND THE WORLD

There are several factors that determine the distribution of animals. Plate tectonics, land bridges, and island biogeography all contribute to why certain animals appear where they do.

Plate tectonics is a result of the energy contained in the Earth and acts as the changing force responsible for our world as we see it today. The elements of plate tectonics and time contribute to not only the evolution of life, but of the Earth itself. The distribution of organisms throughout Earth's history is a direct result of the interaction of energy and tectonics.

The Earth is a layered planet consisting of the crust, mantle, and core. The outer 62 miles (100 km) is a rigid layer called the lithosphere, which is made up of the crust and uppermost mantle. The lithosphere is broken into a number of large and small plates that move over the asthenosphere—a "plastic" layer in the upper mantle. Earthquakes and volcanoes are concentrated at the boundaries between lithospheric plates. These plates move at a rate of a few inches, or centimeters, per year which is about the same rate that human fingernails grow.

There are three types of plate boundaries—convergent boundaries, divergent boundaries, and transform fault boundaries. Convergent boundaries occur when two plates come together. If one plate is under the ocean and collides with a plate that is a continent, the ocean plate will dive beneath the continental plate in a "subduction zone." A divergent boundary occurs when two plates move away from each other. This is common on the ocean floor and is what forms the deep ocean trenches. A transform fault is where two plates slide past each other going in opposite directions.

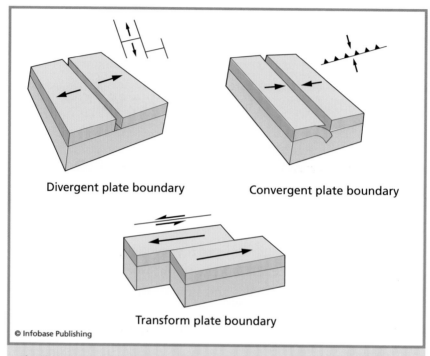

Divergent plate boundary   Convergent plate boundary

Transform plate boundary

© Infobase Publishing

The three types of plate boundaries: divergent, convergent, and transform.

The idea that the continents move is an old one; Alfred Wegener, a German meteorologist, proposed the theory of continental drift in the early 1900s. He believed that at one time the Earth had only one supercontinent, called Pangaea. Over geologic time, as shown in the illustration on page 37, this continent was thought to have broken up, and the individual pieces moved away from each other. He based his theory on several observations: (1) the similarity in shape of the continents—they looked like a giant jigsaw puzzle that could be fit together; (2) the presence of glacial deposits on continents now found near the equator; (3) the presence of certain fossils that all exist on the now widely separated continents of Africa, Australia, and India; and (4) the similarity of rock sequences on different continents.

Then in the 1960s, an American geologist named Harry Hess proposed the theory of sea-floor spreading, in which basaltic magma

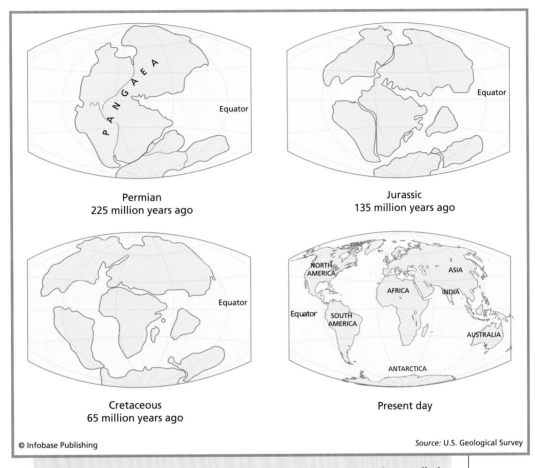

Permian
225 million years ago

Jurassic
135 million years ago

Cretaceous
65 million years ago

Present day

© Infobase Publishing   *Source:* U.S. Geological Survey

All landmasses were once combined at the equator in a supercontinent called Pangaea. Over geologic time, the land mass broke apart and drifted across the Earth to eventually end up where the continents are today.

from the mantle rises to create new ocean floor at mid-ocean ridges—a theory that has since been proved through the study of the age of the ocean floor in different parts of the ocean (it is youngest at the mid-ocean ridges and gets progressively older the farther away from the mid-ocean ridge it is). With this discovery, the theories of continental drift and sea-floor spreading were combined into the theory of plate tectonics—the movement of the various plates around the Earth.

From an evolutionary and ecological perspective, continental drift is significant because it explains some basic patterns of similarity and dissimilarity of plant and animal life around the world. Until about 200 million years ago, all the continents were clustered together at the equator—so even Antarctica was home to tropical plants and animals at one time.

Because the various plates that formed Pangaea broke apart at different times—millions of years apart—each plate carried a different set of life-forms that developed their own unique evolutionary history. As each breakaway piece pulled free of the main landmass, the organisms living on the two parts were separated. From that moment on, the population on the mainland and that on the breakaway piece followed different evolutionary tracks.

The result was that the continents that separated first have had the longest evolutionary isolation and have the most unusual, or diverse, collections of species. Those continents that separated relatively recently—such as South America and Africa, have the most evolutionary history in common and show the most similarity in their plants and animals.

There is much evidence to support these theories of the distribution of life. Scientists think that because Australia separated from the other landmasses fairly early, mammal diversity was still very low. Australian life-forms consisted of monotremes (egg-laying mammals like the platypuses) and marsupials (mammals that raise their young in a pouch, such as kangaroos). For millions of years, there were no other mammals in Australia. Then, when Australia's northward drift caused it to move toward southeast Asia 16 million years ago, rodents, such as rats and bats, managed to cross to Australia and establish populations—but, for over 50 million years, Australia was dominated by marsupials.

Areas like South America and Australia, which was one of the last continents to separate, have many similarities in their plants and animals. Since separation, their animal species have continued to independently adapt, but scientists do find common genetic roots between them.

Land bridges are another mechanism that can help determine the distribution of animals. When sea levels lower, land that had previously been covered by water can become exposed as the ocean level declines. When these land bridges are present, species can walk across them to other locations. For example, scientists believe that the Bering Land Bridge that existed between Alaska and Russia when the sea level was lower was used by many species—such as Siberian huskies and even humans—to migrate from Russia to North America. After the sea level rose, the land bridge disappeared beneath the ocean.

Islands have been a prime target for the study of animal (and plant) adaptation. By their very nature, islands are isolated and serve as a type of living laboratory of evolution. Animals and plants can arrive on islands by being carried on air currents during storms or by ocean currents. When a species becomes isolated on an island, it adapts to the conditions there, and species can evolve that are *endemic*—they only exist on that particular island. Scientists have studied the richness of endemic species on islands such as the Hawaiian Islands, the Galapagos Islands, and the Canary Islands. Oftentimes, when a species has evolved and adapted to a specific niche, it can be at risk of endangerment or extinction when humans introduce other species to the island, which

The Fate of the Passenger Pigeon

In the early 1800s and before, flocks of passenger pigeons were so big they used to darken the sky in the eastern part of North America. It was estimated that there were billions of them. Because of their sheer numbers, many hunters shot them to sell as food. Other people hunted them just for the sport of it.

Unfortunately, because they nested in dense colonies, passenger pigeons were extremely easy to kill in large numbers. So many people were killing them that, by the end of the 1800s, their populations started becoming small. In 1914, the last known passenger pigeon died in the Cincinnati Zoo.

can outcompete the native animals. This has already happened to several endemic species in the Hawaiian Islands.

THE COSTS AND REALITY OF EXTINCTION

Extinction refers to both the disappearance of prehistoric life-forms as well as the more recent ones. Many things can affect the survival of a particular species—continental drift, climatic change, volcanoes, and meteor impacts. These factors are natural and cannot be controlled. In fact, since life began, about 99% of the Earth's species have disappeared, and, on at least five occasions, huge numbers have died out in mass extinctions over a relatively short period of time. Despite natural catastrophes, the total number of living species has, until recently, followed an upward trend.

Today, the extinction rate is increasing more rapidly—up to 1,000 times faster than the natural rate. Many of the more recent extinctions are a direct result of human actions. As the world's population increases, animals' natural habitats are destroyed to make way for humans. At other times, animals are hunted to extinction by humans.

Extinct, Endangered, and Vulnerable Animal Species

Class	Critically endangered	Endangered	Vulnerable	Total threatened	Extinct
Mammals	169	315	612	1,096	119
Birds	168	235	704	1,107	108
Reptiles	41	59	153	253	21
Amphibians	18	31	75	124	5
Insects	44	116	377	537	73
Other animals	471	423	1,194	2,088	343

(Statistics courtesy of the World Conservation Union)

In Africa, uncontrolled hunting and poaching has become a serious problem since animals—such as elephants and rhinoceroses—are killed for their ivory tusks.

Species that are few in number are referred to as *endangered species*. These species will likely become extinct unless humans take action to prevent it. Extinction occurs when the death rate of a species is greater than the birthrate for an extended period of time.

There are millions of life-forms that humans depend on for their own existence. But they don't have to die out, because people can take steps to protect them and help biodiversity for the future. For example, humans can stop the destruction of animal habitats and try to repair as much of the damage as possible through reforesting areas and conserving resources.

The number of animal species that are endangered or extinct is summarized in the table on page 40, although these numbers continue to rise.

As will be seen in Chapter 7, many governments understand the problem and are concerned about the effects of overuse, endangerment, and extinction. Many governments have made hunting and trading various animals illegal and have set up endangered species lists in order to protect animals from extinction.

3

RENEWABLE AND NONRENEWABLE RESOURCES

There are two general classes of resources: renewable and nonrenewable. This chapter focuses on how energy flows through an ecosystem, the importance of food webs to animal survival, and the important physical cycles that affect animals and their relationship with the environment. If these critical cycles remain in balance, then the needs of the system are met and resources don't become endangered. Finally, this chapter focuses on wild mustangs in the American West and why they are considered living legends.

TYPES OF RESOURCES

A renewable resource is a resource that can be replenished. It is a resource that can be replaced through natural ecological cycles or good management practices. The opposite of this is a nonrenewable resource—a resource that cannot be replenished (once it is gone, it is gone forever). For practical applications, some scientists consider a renewable resource one that can be replenished within one generation (approximately 20–30 years).

For many classes of resources, it is easy to determine which resources are renewable and which are not. For example, in the case of energy resources, fossil fuels (oil and petroleum) and coal are not renewable because they took millions of years to form. Even though the same geological forces are still active today, these resources—which were formed from the remains of dinosaurs and ancient vegetation millions of years ago—will never be replaced within our lifetime. Energy resources, such as wind power and waterpower are considered renewable because they are readily abundant and can be generated within a short period of time.

Ecosystems are complex and fragile. All elements of living systems are interwoven; if one element is affected, the entire system is affected. Animal life is a highly valuable resource, and humans depend on animals daily. They play a significant role in having a healthy ecosystem. Without animals, people would not have food and certain medicines as well as some types of clothes, industrial products, and other valuable resources.

If the environment is not cared for, animal habitats can be easily impacted. If their habitats are destroyed, if their air is polluted, if they are overhunted, or if part of their food web is destroyed, animal species can become threatened.

As covered earlier, natural forces such as climatic change, earthquakes, floods, drought, volcanoes, and meteor impacts can also threaten and endanger animals. Once an animal is threatened, it is in danger of becoming extinct. The conditions causing the threat of extinction need to be fixed. If they are not, and more individuals of a species die than are born, the animal could become extinct. Once an animal has become extinct, it is gone forever, and that animal has become a nonrenewable resource—such as the dinosaurs, the dodo, and the passenger pigeon.

If the situation threatening a species' health and existence is reversed, then—with care—it is possible to increase their numbers, regenerate the failing population, and bring it out of danger. It takes the efforts of scientists, conservationists, ecologists, and private citizens to make sure an animal's ecosystem remains healthy. Everyone can play an active role in this endeavor.

ENERGY FLOW THROUGH THE ECOSYSTEM

Energy flows through the ecosystem in a specific way. Balanced ecosystems can be affected by human activities. For example, if pollution is introduced into the system, it will move through the system in a specific way, harming many components of the ecosystem.

Organisms can either be **producers** or **consumers**. Producers take energy from the environment—such as the sun—and convert it into carbon bonds, such as sugar. Plants are the most common producers. They take energy from sunlight and convert carbon dioxide into glucose (or other sugars) through photosynthesis. Algae and cyanobacteria also produce energy through photosynthesis. The bacteria that thrive around deep-sea vents are also producers, because they take energy from chemicals coming from inside the Earth and convert it to sugars. Other bacteria living deep underground are also producers. Another term for producers is *autotrophs*.

Consumers get their energy from the carbon bonds made by producers. Another term for consumers is *heterotrophs*. Based on what they eat, there are four groups of heterotrophs (see table below).

Groups of Heterotrophs

Consumer	Trophic level	Food source
Herbivores	Primary	Plants
Carnivores	Secondary or higher	Animals
Omnivores	All levels	Plants and animals
Detritivores	All levels	Detritus

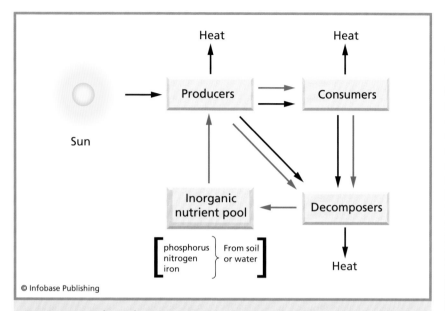

Energy moves through an ecosystem in the form of carbon-carbon bonds. The process of respiration breaks the carbon-carbon bonds. Carbon is then combined with oxygen to form carbon dioxide. This process releases the energy, which is either used by the animal, or the energy may be lost as heat. All energy comes from the sun and all energy in ecosystems is eventually lost as heat. Inorganic nutrients do not contain carbon-carbon bonds. The movement of inorganic nutrients through an ecosystem is noted above by the red arrows. Unlike energy, inorganic nutrients are recycled.

The trophic level refers to the animal's position in the food chain. Autotrophs are at the base because they produce the food. Organisms that eat the autotrophs are called herbivores or primary consumers. An example of an herbivore is a grazing animal such as a cow, horse, deer, or giraffe.

An organism that eats herbivores is a carnivore and a secondary consumer. A carnivore that eats another carnivore that eats an herbivore is called a tertiary consumer, and so on. Animals that eat both plants and animals—such as humans—are called **omnivores**. Most carnivores don't limit their diet to organisms of only one trophic level.

Energy flows through a system utilizing producers, consumers, and **decomposers** as shown in the illustration on page 45. In this energy flow, energy and inorganic nutrients from the soil and water—such as phosphorous, nitrogen, and iron—move through the system. The energy is flowing as carbon-carbon bonds. The carbon bonds are broken down and converted to carbon dioxide. This process releases the energy, which is either used by the organism (to move, think, eat, digest, and so on) or lost as heat.

An interesting point to note is that energy does not recycle. It begins as sunshine, and it is all finally spent as heat. As one organism is consumed by another, the inorganic nutrients are passed from organism to organism. In the end, all organisms eventually die and become detritus—food for the decomposers. The last of the energy is lost as heat, and the inorganic nutrients are returned to the soil or water, and the process starts again. In this way, inorganic nutrients are recycled, although energy is not.

FOOD WEBS—FEEDING EVERYONE

Every living thing needs energy to remain alive. A food chain is a simple way of looking at how that energy is transferred from one living thing to another. A food chain is the path of food from a given final consumer back to a producer. A simple food chain may start with grasses and seeds, which are eaten by a field mouse, which is eaten by a gopher snake, which is finally eaten by a red-tailed hawk. In real life, however, an organism doesn't usually stick with just one food source—it eats a varied diet of many components. Scientists use food webs to study the interactions between many animals from producers to consumers. Food webs demonstrate the complexity of the interdependence of living things within a habitat.

The elimination of the smallest link in the food chain can upset the delicate balance of nature's food supplies. Typically, in a food web, the producer is on the bottom, and the final consumers are at the top. A food web consists of interlocking food chains. The only

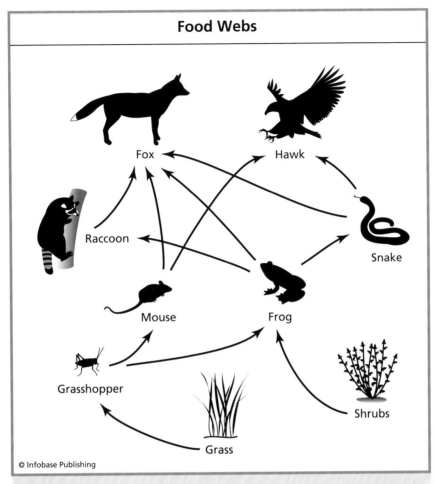

Food Webs

Fox

Hawk

Raccoon

Snake

Mouse

Frog

Grasshopper

Shrubs

Grass

© Infobase Publishing

Food webs show the complexity of an ecosystem. If one element is missing, it can have a far-reaching effect on the rest of the ecosystem.

way to untangle the chains is to trace back along a given food chain to its source.

Human civilization is dependent on agriculture. Because of this, the food web for humans differs from other natural food chains. In agriculture, the environment must be manipulated to grow the plant species people eat. For example, farmers plant crops and seek to get rid of weeds. The human food web generally has three levels—producers (crops), primary consumers (livestock and humans), and secondary consumers (humans). In this food pyramid, little energy is lost between trophic levels because there are only three levels involved.

Agricultural ecosystems—although convenient for humans—do have associated problems, however. When only one crop is planted, a monoculture has been created. The negative side of this is that when a large number of similar plants are confined to a small area, this increases the chances for disease and insects to destroy the plants. This is why it takes a lot of chemicals (pesticides) to keep a monoculture operating.

The concept of biomass is important in food webs. In general, the higher an organism is in the trophic level (the further away from the source), the less biomass it will contain. In general, about 10% of the energy available in one trophic level will be passed on to the next. Therefore, each trophic level will weigh only about 10% of the level below it and 10 times as much as the level above it. For example, one bald eagle (at the top of the web) had to eat a lot of snakes to survive; each of those snakes had to eat a lot of mice and grasshoppers; and those mice and grasshoppers had to eat a lot of grass. Therefore, it ultimately took the consumption of all the grass, grasshoppers, mice, and snakes to feed the eagle. This concept is referred to as a food pyramid.

Biological magnification is another important concept. It is the tendency of pollutants to become concentrated in successive trophic levels. This is bad for the organisms up the food chain because the pollutants get concentrated, and they are often toxic. The pollutants are usually introduced into the food web at the bottom of the food chain—for example, in the surrounding soil or water plants grow in.

Producers take in inorganic nutrients from their surroundings. Problems occur when a pollutant—such as **DDT** or mercury—is present in the environment. Chemically, these pollutants are mixed in with the essential inorganic nutrients and are brought into the producer by mistake and stored. This represents the first step of biomagnification.

Bald eagles were almost eliminated due to widespread use of the pesticide DDT. A ban on DDT use has led to an increase in the number of bald eagles, although they still remain an endangered species. *(Courtesy of U.S. Fish & Wildlife Service, Steve Hillebrand)*

At this point, the pollutant is at a higher concentration inside the producer than it is in the environment.

When a consumer obtains its food from a lower level, it is also consuming large amounts of the pollutant. Therefore, when pollutants biomagnify, they are absorbed and stored in the bodies of the consumers. This often happens with pollutants soluble in fat such as DDT or **PCB**s. These materials are digested from the producer and moved into the fat of the consumer. If the consumer is caught and eaten, its fat is digested, and the pollutant moves to the fat of the new consumer, and so on. In this way, the pollutant builds up in the fatty tissues of the consumers.

One of the most well-known examples of biomagnification is the use of DDT. DDT is a pesticide, and its use has improved human health in many countries by killing insects, such as disease-spreading mosquitoes. One of the reasons DDT was thought to make a good pesticide is that it doesn't break down in the environment, but because of this, it is ingested by organisms and stored in their fat.

In some species, DDT has proved to be extremely harmful. The most well-known example is the effect DDT has had on birds. In birds, DDT interferes with the deposition of calcium in the shells of the birds' eggs. The resulting eggs are then very soft and easily broken. After a while, species of birds were unable to produce young, and their existence suddenly became endangered. This is what threatened the existence of bald eagles.

Because of this, the use of DDT was banned in the United States in the 1960s, and a large environmental protection movement by American citizens was begun—a good example of what becoming involved in animal protection can do. Fortunately, the bald eagle has made a comeback as a result of banning DDT in the United States.

BIOGEOCHEMICAL CYCLES—MAINTAINING A DELICATE BALANCE

The inorganic nutrients in an ecosystem cycle through more than just the organisms. They also enter into the atmosphere, the oceans, the ground, and rocks. Because the chemicals cycle through the biological world (living things) and the geological, or physical, world (the oceans, land, and atmosphere), the cycles that affect ecosystems are often referred to as biogeochemical cycles.

Each chemical is unique and has its own properties, but all of the cycles share things in common. When chemicals are held in storage for long periods of time, they are contained in reservoirs. When a chemical is not held in a particular place for a long time—but moves through the system faster—the chemicals are in exchange pools.

The amount of time a chemical is held in an exchange pool or a reservoir is called its residence time. In the case of water, when water is stored in groundwater or the oceans, it is in a reservoir because it stays there for a long time. When water is in the form of rain, snow, or a cloud, it is in an exchange pool because it remains in that part of its cycle for a relatively short time.

The biotic community in an ecosystem includes all the living organisms, large and small. The biotic system serves to move chemicals from one stage to another. For example, the water that trees use from the ground is then evaporated into the atmosphere. The sun and the heat from the mantle and core of the Earth are what provide most of the energy to transport the chemicals. The most important biogeo-chemical cycles in ecosystems are the water, carbon, nitrogen, and phosphorous cycles.

The Water Cycle

Water is necessary for animal survival, plant growth, for dissolving and transporting plant nutrients, and for the survival of soil organisms. The water cycle is fundamental to all living things on Earth.

From a fast-moving stream to rainfall to movement of water through the ground, water is always in motion. The endless movement and recycling of water between the atmosphere, the land's surface, and underground is called the water cycle, or the hydrologic cycle.

Two separate forces make the water cycle work: The energy of the sun and the force of the Earth's gravity. Water vapor is carried through the atmosphere by air currents. When the air cools, it condenses, forming clouds. Some of the moisture falls back to Earth as rain, snow, hail, or sleet.

Once the water reaches the ground, it can go in several directions before it returns again to the atmosphere. Animals and plants can use the water. It can also be stored in lakes, or it can seep into the soil. The sun's energy can then make the water evaporate back into the atmosphere, or the Earth's gravity can pull the water that has entered the ground down through the soil to be stored for years as slowly moving groundwater.

Groundwater can be stored in aquifers (natural underground reservoirs), or it can eventually seep into springs and resurface. Water on the surface is returned to the atmosphere through the process of evaporation. Water that has been used by plants is returned to the atmosphere as vapor through transpiration, which happens when water passes through the leaves of plants. These two concepts together are called *evapotranspiration*. Evapotranspiration is greatest in areas that are hot, dry, sunny, or windy.

Although water is critical for animal survival, plant growth, and the transporting of nutrients, it can also be a destructive force if not managed properly. It can cause soil compaction, which clumps the particles of soil close together and removes the important air space needed for nutrients to move through the soil; it can leach (remove) nutrients from the soil; and too much water can cause excess runoff and erosion.

The Carbon Cycle

The carbon cycle is important because carbon is the basic structural material for all cell life. Carbon makes the soil productive and plants healthy. The carbon cycle is the movement of carbon between the atmosphere, the oceans, the land, and living organisms.

The atmosphere and plants exchange carbon. Plants absorb carbon dioxide from the atmosphere during photosynthesis and then release carbon dioxide back into the atmosphere during respiration.

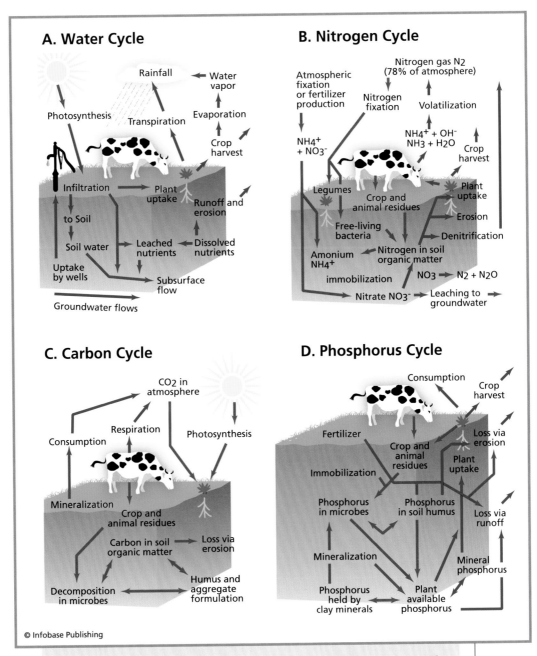

A. Water Cycle

B. Nitrogen Cycle

C. Carbon Cycle

D. Phosphorus Cycle

© Infobase Publishing

Biogeochemical cycles: (a) The Water Cycle; (b) The Nitrogen Cycle; (c) The Carbon Cycle; (d) The Phosphorus Cycle

Another major exchange of carbon dioxide happens between the ocean and the atmosphere. The dissolved carbon dioxide in the oceans is used by ocean plants in photosynthesis.

Carbon is also exchanged through the soil. Crop and animal residues decompose and form organic matter, which contains carbon. For plants to be able to use these nutrients, soil organisms break them down in a process called mineralization.

Animals also give off carbon dioxide when they breathe. Some plants are eaten by grazing animals, which then return organic carbon to the soil as manure. Easily broken-down forms of carbon in manure and plant cells are released as carbon dioxide. Forms of carbon that are difficult to break down become stabilized in the soil as humus.

The Nitrogen Cycle

The nitrogen cycle is the process by which nitrogen in the atmosphere enters the soil and becomes part of living organisms before returning to the atmosphere. Nitrogen makes up 78% of the Earth's atmosphere. But this nitrogen must be converted from a gas into a chemically usable form before living organisms can use it. This transformation takes place through the nitrogen cycle. It transforms the nitrogen gas into ammonia or nitrates.

Most of the nitrogen conversion process is done biologically by free-living, nitrogen-fixing bacteria; bacteria living on the roots of plants; and through certain algae and lichens.

Nitrogen that has been converted to ammonia and nitrates is used directly by plants and is absorbed in their tissues as plant proteins. The nitrogen then passes from plants to herbivores and then to carnivores.

When plants and animals die, the nitrogen compounds are broken down by decomposing into ammonia. Some of this ammonia is then used by plants, and the rest is either dissolved or held in the soil. If it is dissolved or held in the soil, microorganisms then go to work on it in a process called nitrification. The nitrates made from this process can be stored in humus or washed from the soil and carried away to streams and lakes. Nitrates may also be converted and returned to the atmosphere by a process called dentrification.

The nitrogen cycle is important because plants need nitrogen to grow, develop, and produce seeds. The main source of nitrogen in soils

Bald Eagles

Range: United States, Canada, northwest Mexico
Habitat: Coastlines, lakes, rivers, swamps, and marshes
Scientific name: *Haliaeetus leucocephalus*
Body length: 29–42 inches (74–107 cm)
Wingspan: 5.5–8 feet (1.7–2.4 m)
Weight: Males 6–9 pounds (2.7–4 kg), females 10–15 pounds (4.5–6.8 kg)
Life span: 25–40 years
Number of eggs laid: 1–3
Incubation: 35 days
Age of maturity: 4 years
Conservation status: Threatened

The bald eagle is America's national symbol, signifying strength, power, and freedom. They live near bodies of water to be close to their favorite food—fish. Bald eagles can see four to seven times better than humans. This helps them spot prey (food). A bald eagle is a bird of prey. Unlike human eyes, an eagle's eyes can't move from side to side, requiring the eagle to turn its whole head to see a wide range.

Bald eagles mate for life. Both parents help care for the chicks, called eaglets. The bald eagle is an excellent nest builder. A pair will make a large nest high in a tree and come back to it year after year, adding more twigs, grass, moss, feathers, and branches to the original nest until it becomes huge.

Bald eagles are at the top of the food chain, so they have no natural enemies—except humans. A bald eagle can reach a speed of 200 miles per hour (322 km/hr) when diving through the air hunting prey. When a bald eagle loses a feather on one wing, it will lose a matching one on the other so that its balance is not adversely affected.

is from organic matter (humus). Bacteria that live in the soil convert organic forms of nitrogen to inorganic forms that plants can use. Nitrogen is then taken up by plant roots. When the plant dies, it decays and becomes part of the organic matter in the soil. The land must be well managed, or nitrogen can be washed out of the soil.

The Phosphorus Cycle

Like nitrogen, phosphorus is a primary plant nutrient. But phosphorus is not part of the atmosphere. It is found in rocks, minerals, and organic matter in the soil. Chemical reactions and activity by microbes (microorganisms) in the soil affect the availability of phosphorus for plants to use.

Plants use phosphorus for energy and reproduction. Animals consume phosphorus when they eat plants. The phosphorus that is not used to help the animal grow is returned to the soil in the animal's manure. Once the phosphorus is in the soil again, it is decomposed by soil organisms so that it can be used by plants again, and the cycle repeats itself.

WILD MUSTANGS—PROTECTING A VALUABLE AMERICAN RESOURCE

Although wild horses became extinct in North America 8,000 years ago, they were reintroduced back in the days of Columbus and Cortez, the Italian and Spanish explorers who brought horses to North America.

Horses quickly became an integral part of the American West. They were used to pull wagons, help build the railroads, carry mail along the Pony Express trail, and plow fields. Many descendants of these domesticated horses escaped and lived life free. Even more were abandoned by settlers, ranchers, mining prospectors, Native American tribes, and the U.S. cavalry between the late 1800s and 1930s, forming the first wild horse herds.

Wild horses are a true living legend of the American West. They are naturally athletic and extremely intelligent. Of no particular **breed**, their

Wild mustangs run free in Utah. These horses are rugged, hearty, and resilient. *(Courtesy of the U.S. Bureau of Land Management, Kelly Rigby)*

colors are as diverse as their attitudes and abilities. Some say wild horses are born in the colors of the western mountains and snowcapped peaks.

As a result of harsh environmental demands and adaptive growth, wild horses possess stronger legs, higher bone density, and harder hooves than domestic horses. The fitness these horses require for survival in the wild is comparable to the level of fitness an Olympic athlete needs in grueling cross-country events.

Then misfortune struck. Beginning in the 1920s and continuing through the 1950s, some people saw the wild horse herds as a means to make a quick dollar. "Mustangers," as they came to be called, captured and sold them for pet food. This enraged those who considered these majestic animals to represent the spirit of the West, causing public outcry in the late 1960s.

The efforts of Nevada's Velma Johnston (also called "Wild Horse Annie") and thousands of school children were instrumental in the passing of laws protecting wild horses. The Wild Free-Roaming Horse and Burro Act of 1971 provided for the protection of wild horses on public lands.

In 1973, the Bureau of Land Management (BLM), an agency of the U.S. Department of the Interior that is entrusted with managing 264 million acres of public lands (located mainly in the western states), was given the responsibility of managing and preserving the wild horse and burro as "living symbols" of the Old West. In 1976, the Adopt-a-Horse program—the BLM's most popular program to date—was born. This program was designed to remove excess wild horses from the range in order to protect and maintain healthy herds and habitat of wild horses for future generations to enjoy.

Since the first horse was offered for adoption in Montana in 1973, the BLM has placed more than 185,000 wild horses into private care. The wild horse program is an example of how—with proper land management and care of the environment—the health and welfare of wildlife can be maintained, protected, and preserved.

DEVELOPMENT AND THE RESULTING CONSEQUENCES

The last chapter illustrated the impacts of agriculture on wildlife habitat. This chapter explores further development of the land for humans' wants and needs, such as urbanization, ranching, and recreation. It explores the concept of multiple uses of the land and why responsible land management is important for the health of all animals—including people—now and in the future. It focuses on the modern-day approach and how computers and other technological tools are helping managers and researchers care for the land more efficiently.

DEVELOPMENT OF THE LAND AND ITS EFFECTS

An abundance of wildlife can survive where there is a large amount of wild, undeveloped places and intact wildlife habitat. Before rapid exploration and settlement began in the western United States, huge herds of buffalo—also called bison—roamed the open ranges.

When people began moving into the area and converting wide-open cores of buffalo habitat to urban use by building houses and

Buffalo (also called bison) live in a prairie ecosystem. These North American mammals were once plentiful but were over-hunted and became endangered. Very few free-roaming buffalo exist today. *(Courtesy of the U.S. Dept of Agriculture, Keith Weller)*

roads, it began to affect the natural habitat for the wildlife. Settlers also began hunting and killing the buffalo, eliminating large herds of these animals. They were hunted so extensively that today there are very few buffalo left.

The same types of human impact are still happening today as more land is developed for human use. Wildlife needs large core areas of natural habitat in order to survive and flourish. Some of these core areas of habitat are currently protected because the U.S. government has set aside these areas as national parks and wilderness areas. **Conservation** biologists have proved time and time again that protecting large areas of wild habitat—or cores—is essential to the long-term health of wildlife populations.

Human recreational pursuits can negatively impact wildlife. Ski resorts remove needed vegetation and introduce so much activity that animals are often forced to relocate to a different area. As the animals' areas of inhabitation become smaller and smaller, they become threatened and endangered. *(Nature's Images)*

A major problem with developing urban areas within principal wildlife areas is that animals' habitat becomes fragmented—instead of having a large natural area to live in, animals must survive in smaller, separated segments, or isolated "islands" of habitat. This resulting fragmentation of habitat through the development of areas for roads, houses, and other human activities will eventually encourage extinction of species. One solution to remedy this is to develop wildlife migration corridors, a concept that will be discussed later in this chapter.

As the surface of the land is altered for human use, impacts to wildlife are inevitable. When ranchers maintain herds of cattle on rangeland, they fence in their properties to keep the livestock contained. This, however, keeps wildlife out of the area, and that wildlife no longer has access to the food sources they once relied on in the area.

Recreation is another use of the land that can have a detrimental effect on wildlife. Ski resorts can disturb wildlife migration and feeding habits by eliminating possible food sources as well as introducing noise

A manatee swims off the coast of Florida. These friendly animals often get seriously injured when they venture too close to boat propellers. *(Courtesy of the U.S. Fish & Wildlife Service, Jim P. Reid)*

and activity into a previously peaceful area. Boating and other recreation activities around shorelines have threatened the health of aquatic wildlife. For example, the manatee—a gentle marine animal—has been heavily impacted by the increase in boating and fishing traffic. These docile, friendly animals venture too close to piers and busy harbors and are often injured in boat propeller accidents.

Urbanization is one of the most detrimental impacts of all. As towns and cities spread outward, the native wildlife habitat is impacted. When homes and roads are built, the natural vegetation is often clear-cut (removed) from the area. This eliminates sources of food for wildlife. The presence of roads also presents a major problem, as we will see later in this chapter.

Examples of urbanization and the destruction of natural habitat include: (a) Ground being cleared prior to the construction of new homes in Park City, Utah; (b) Homes already completed near Jordanelle Reservoir, Utah. Notice the removal of vegetation in order to build homes, the ski lift, and the bare soil areas where vegetation was removed to build a road. Once the vegetation is removed, it increases erosion and keeps vegetation from regrowing. Both of these areas are prime habitat for deer, elk, moose, fox, raccoons, and many other types of native animals. Destroying the natural vegetation and building roads threatens the livelihood of native wildlife. *(Nature's Images, Julie A. Kerr)*

Once housing replaces natural habitat and the native plant species are removed, other nonnative plant species (plants that do not naturally grow in an area) are introduced. These plants are called invasive species. Invasive species can then compete with the existing native vegetation. Because invasive species have not been there long enough to have natural enemies, they can often grow out of control and spread. Not only can this growth be destructive to the native vegetation, but it can also harm animals if it is poisonous or the animals simply do not like it. In this way, it has removed a food source, which then threatens the health and future of the habitat.

Oftentimes, people that have moved into a wildlife habitat area get upset when the wildlife begins eating the landscaping—flowers, bushes,

The construction of homes around pre-existing wildlife habitat often results in conflict between humans and native animals. In the case of the beaver, landowners often get upset when the beaver does what is natural to it: (a) Trees cut down by beavers to be used in the construction of dams; (b) A tree recently cut down by a beaver. The marks of the beaver's strong front teeth are visible in the wood. *(Nature's Images, Julie A. Kerr)*

shrubs, and trees planted in their yards. For example, deer, elk, and moose commonly do this. Sometimes people do not stop to realize that the animal is simply trying to exist in its previous habitat. People that build near streams—in areas called riparian areas—often have their landscaping destroyed by beavers. The beaver, however, is simply living in its environment the way it always has.

These are good illustrations of why accommodating wildlife is important. Some people who live in traditional deer habitat areas choose to landscape their yards with vegetation that the deer like to browse on (eat). This can help tremendously in the harsh winter months. The higher elevations—where the deer usually spend their summers—become inaccessible in the snow, and food becomes scarce. Deer herds move downslope into the foothills and valley bottoms. If houses have been built there—in what is called their winter range—it can be devastating to herds, and many deer will starve.

THE CONCEPT OF MULTIPLE USES

With so much demand placed on the land for both human and wildlife needs, it is critical that resources and the land be managed effectively so that habitats do not become diminished or changed adversely. There are many possible uses of the land, and many of them overlap. For example, some areas may be suitable for wildlife habitat; recreational activities such as camping, backpacking, and hiking; mining commodities, such as gold, silver, limestone, copper, and many other elements; and logging—cutting down trees to use in the timber industry for construction and firewood.

Urbanization, as mentioned, is a significant use of the land. Accompanying this is the construction of hundreds of miles of roads. Railways can be constructed, as well as power lines and pipelines for electricity, gas, and water. These areas are usually surrounded by buffers called rights-of-way. Agricultural development is another major multiple-use impact. Although necessary for human survival, growing crops has its impacts. Not only does it replace the native vegetation, but monocultures—growing only one crop on a piece of land—lowers biodiversity, reduces nutrients in the soil, and can cause erosion. It also increases the risk of disease. If a crop is infected by a disease, it can destroy the entire crop. In areas with a mixture of different plants, the rate of survival is naturally higher because not all types of plants may be harmed by a particular disease.

Hunting is another use of the land introduced by humans. Without effective limits and restrictions from proper management, species could be hunted to extinction, as was the case with the passenger pigeon.

In areas where water is a resource, such as streams, rivers, reservoirs, wetlands, lakes, and oceans, there can be conflict between the aquatic

River Rafting is a popular summertime activity, as demonstrated above by a group of adventure seekers on the Colorado River. Humans must, however, be cautious and mindful of animal habitat that exists in the river and along its banks so that it is not adversely impacted. *(Courtesy of the U.S. Bureau of Land Management, Kelly Rigby)*

wildlife and recreation. Activities that compete with wildlife include river rafting, fishing, boating, water skiing, and scuba diving.

If humans are not mindful of the wildlife they are sharing the land with, there can be substantial impacts. For example, polluting water bodies can destroy the habitats of fish and other aquatic animals. Polluting the water can involve chemicals, garbage, or even dumping too much sediment into waterways from construction and erosion. It is not only dangerous to the wildlife, but also impacts the food supply for people, as well.

Many birds use wetland areas as nesting sites. Polluting or destroying wetlands takes away a crucial area needed by many birds for survival. Another threat to wildlife concerns introduced animal species. When humans move into an area and bring other animals with them, it can have a long-lasting effect on the native species. For example, introducing dogs into a woodland area becomes a threat to smaller animals such as rabbits, mice, squirrels, and chipmunks, because they can be hunted and eaten by the dogs.

In some island areas, animals have been introduced. Because islands are relatively isolated places, their endemic species adapt to their habitats. Then, if a competitive animal is introduced, the endemic species can die off from being hunted directly or from being unable to compete for food and then starving. Introduced species can also introduce new diseases that the native species have never been exposed to.

The Gray Wolf

Gray wolves (*Canis lupus*) are rare and endangered in much of their range in the Rocky Mountains and were listed under the Endangered Species Act in 1973. The habitat range of wolves has shrunk considerably over the past 300 years because they have been hunted extensively by people. The gray wolf has made a comeback, however, through the reintroduction of wolves into Yellowstone National Park.

Wolves travel and live in packs. They come in a variety of colors, ranging from pure white to solid black, although most have a grizzled gray-brown color. They have very thick coats that consist of two layers—a soft, insulating undercoat and long **guard hairs** that help keep them dry.

Wolves are carnivores. They hunt and eat large mammals, such as deer. They once occupied a vast array of habitats in the temperate, subtropical, and desert areas. Now, however, they exist mainly in the northern forests and Arctic tundra. A wolf pack's **territory** can cover anywhere from 20 to 120 square miles (52 to 310 sq. km).

Because native species have no natural defenses against new diseases, they can become sick and die. All these issues have to be considered by scientists and land managers, and plans need to be put in place to protect all forms of threatened and endangered organisms.

RESPONSIBLE LAND MANAGEMENT

Due to the multiple-use concept of land management it is extremely important that land managers make well-informed decisions. There are many pressures on the land that need to be managed—logging, road building, off-road vehicle use and other motorized recreation, and wildfires. One major problem the western United States has faced is long-term drought. This condition causes the vegetation to dry out. If the humidity is low and the winds are strong when a wildfire starts (usually by a lightning strike, but sometimes by people), it can be highly destructive to wildlife habitat.

According to the U.S. Forest Service, there are currently over 380,000 miles of roads on America's national forests—eight times the combined length of the interstate highway system. In addition to miles of roads on these public lands, off-road vehicle use is increasing at an alarming rate and poses one of the fastest-growing threats to our wild lands. These off-road vehicles (ORVs)—also referred to as all-terrain vehicles (ATVs)—with their growing popularity and technological advances (in combination with poor land management practices in some areas), are creating a web of trails on the natural landscape. ATVs, built to travel across rugged land-scapes, cause severe disruption to the soil, facilitate the spread of invasive plant seeds, and disturb sensitive and endangered wildlife.

The most feasible way for managers to effectively manage the land and protect wildlife is to identify habitat core areas and their connect-ing corridors. Wide-ranging wildlife species need secure core habitat where human activity is limited, ecosystem functions are still intact, and wildlife populations are able to flourish. Many species of wildlife encounter areas that are not large enough for long-term health, and they must move from one core area to another. Corridors are areas that connect these core areas, as shown in the illustration on page 70.

Certain outdoor areas have been designated for use of All-Terrain Vehicles (ATVs). Problems can occur when ATVs are driven into places where there is no designated trail. In arid environments, they can damage vegetation and promote erosion, which affects wildlife habitat. The noise can also be intimidating and disruptive to animals. *(Nature's Images)*

Ever since scientists began to recognize that wildlife habitat was becoming more and more fragmented, there has been great interest in the concept of designing reserves and maintaining connectivity between those reserves of wildlife habitat. The purpose of these core areas, corridors, and buffers is to limit human activities and to have the maintenance of wildlife habitat and biodiversity as the primary goals.

These wildlife "reserves" are designed to conserve as much of the natural connectivity as possible in the face of human population growth and development. These reserves are important because the habitat destruction practices of humans reduce the connectivity of

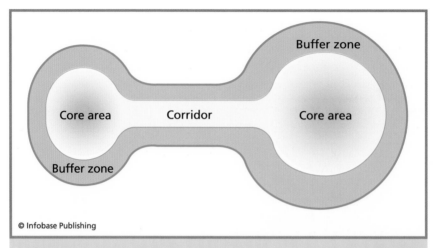

© Infobase Publishing

Core habitats for a particular species may exist in separate areas. For the wildlife to be able to access multiple core areas, it is necessary that a designated corridor be available so that animals can travel from one area to another. The buffer zone is helpful so that wildlife is protected from the impact of people's urban or industrial uses of the land.

habitat for the majority of wildlife species. In many places, a narrow corridor is all that remains to allow for the movement of wildlife.

This type of management is important because landscape-level processes such as wildfire, disease, and hydrologic events (such as floods), have always been a part of this system. Animal movements have been fine-tuned by evolution to function within the natural range of variation existing in the landscape.

Human impact, however, has changed the landscape too rapidly and too extensively for most animals to adapt. Because of this, most animals try to move across landscapes that are often much more hostile than anything they are prepared to encounter. To get from one good habitat island to another, an animal often has to expose itself to predators, travel through areas where there is nothing to eat or drink, or risk getting lost and never finding another secure island of suitable habitat.

A wildlife corridor can function at several scales. It can allow seasonal movements for a species, such as deer, elk, or moose migration, between summer and winter ranges. It can also allow long-term travel corridors for animals that migrate greater distances.

Planning for and managing wildlife corridors encourages conservation-minded management. Another application where sound management is making an impact is with roads and wildlife. Roads and wildlife are a deadly combination for both humans and animals. It is estimated by the U.S. Fish and Wildlife Service, that over a million

Grizzly Bears

The northern Rocky Mountain range in North America is one of the few places in the United States (excluding Alaska) that is home to grizzly bears (*Ursus arctos*). Over 200 years ago, there were more than 100,000 grizzly bears between the Mississippi River and the Pacific Ocean. Now there are less than 1,000 left in the United States—found mainly in the greater Yellowstone and the northern Continental Divide ecosystems. They mainly live in isolated islands of habitat where they face increasing threats from human development and natural disasters, such as wildfires.

Grizzly bear habitat in the continental United States has been reduced to less than 2% of its original range, which is why grizzlies were placed under the protection of the Endangered Species Act in 1975. Much of the grizzly's existing habitat is threatened by fragmentation from roads and other development.

Grizzlies are omnivores—they eat both plants and meat. Their diet consists of insects, rodents, elk, fish, bison, moose, plants, berries, and roots. Grizzly bears need large areas of wild lands in order to survive. Their home typically ranges over an area about 900 square miles (2,331 sq. km) in size and consists of lands with little to no development. For any chance at long-term survival, grizzlies need a population of several thousand bears capable of safely moving along protected wildlife corridors and other large blocks of secure habitat.

(Source: U.S. Fish and Wildlife Service)

vertebrates are killed every day in the United States on roads. Wildlife and roads are also a human safety issue because more than 200 motorists are killed each year in animal-car collisions. The insurance industry has estimated that the annual cost to society for these accidents is more than $200 million.

Roads cause five impacts to wildlife:

- Direct habitat loss where the road is located.
- Associated with roads are other forms of construction such as houses and businesses.
- Habitats become fragmented.
- Animals change their natural behavior to accommodate interference, such as avoiding roads and surrounding lands.
- Hitting animals in vehicles on the road is the number-one way that humans kill wildlife in the United States.

Roads have a significant impact on large carnivores with low reproduction rates, low population densities, and large home ranges, such as grizzly bears, wolves, and mountain lions. Increasingly, the wildlife corridors that animals have traveled for generations are being crosscut by roads and highways traveled by ever more speeding cars and trucks. According to the Humane Society, hundreds of millions of all types of animals die on roadways in the United States each year.

Good management practices take into account these issues when building or renovating roads. Many areas of the country have taken the initiative to try to create a safer environment for animals. For example, some areas in Montana and Wyoming have built wildlife underpasses. Fencing is constructed to channel the wildlife to a particular section of the highway where a tunnel has been built under the road. The wildlife is able to pass safely through the tunnel to the other side of the road.

Other areas have implemented channeled fencing to a few key locations on the road and designated deer crossings (much like a pedestrian crossing). Animals often need to cross busy highways to reach water sources. The problem with this approach is that at specific points the wildlife—such as deer, moose, and elk—must cross the road. Oftentimes, especially at night, drivers do not notice them in time and hit them. Another problem is that once animals are on the road, they don't always immediately cross through the opposing fence opening on the other side of the road, but instead travel along the roadway, which increases their chances of being hit and killed. For new road construction, wildlife managers and conservationists encourage the federal, state, and local decision makers to consider wildlife and their habitat needs so that roads are not placed within key wildlife habitat.

Safe passages apply to aquatic life as well as animals that live on the land. Species like fish and frogs are also affected. Millions of amphibians die every year trying to cross over roadways. Millions of fish are trapped or misdirected by poorly planned bridges and culverts.

The Canadian Lynx

The Canada lynx (Lynx Canadensis), a close cousin to the bobcat, is a forest dwelling cat that historically inhabited coniferous forests of the northeastern United States, the Great Lakes, the Rocky Mountains, and the Cascade Mountains. Due to trapping, habitat loss, and the lynx's sensitivity to humans, there are only a few lynxes left in the United States. In 2000, the Canada lynx was listed as a **threatened species** under the Endangered Species Act.

A lynx is characterized by a "bobbed," or shorter tail, and tufts of hair on the tops of its ears. It has large paws covered with fur to keep it from sinking into deep snow. Their enlarged feet make them highly adapted to hunting snowshoe hares in deep snow. Lynxes are **nocturnal** (awake at night) and active all year.

Lynxes are very secretive and cautious. They usually avoid large open areas and prefer dense forest for cover. They build dens with dead and downed logs, which provide shelter, escape from other predators, and protection from severe weather.

Another concern with wildlife habitat and human activity is maintaining watershed integrity. It is critical to promote and protect healthy watersheds and clean flowing waters. The waterways are not only home to many native coldwater fish, but are also essential to people and communities for drinking water.

Clean water is only possible if a watershed is kept healthy. This means that watersheds must be well managed when urban, rangeland, agricultural, and wild landscape uses all interact in order to prevent pollution and degradation. Conservationists and land managers must focus on entire watersheds—not just small areas within a watershed—because even remote cases of pollution can flow through and contaminate an entire water system.

HIGH-TECH TOOLS TO HELP LAND MANAGERS

Because of all the decisions that land managers must make and all the issues they must take into consideration when providing for wildlife and their habitat, it can quickly become an overwhelming job. Fortunately, technology has advanced far enough that tools have been developed to handle large amounts of interactive data.

The Geographic Information System—or GIS—involves a powerful, complex, computer database that organizes information about a specific location. It creates a computerized map with a potentially unlimited amount of information available for every place on the map. Each category of information is called a "layer" or "theme." One advantage of GIS over paper maps is that many more layers can be stored and easily displayed in various combinations.

The real strength of GIS lies in its potential to assist scientists and land managers in analyzing data and making informed decisions. Stacking themes or layers of information allows new patterns to emerge for scientific consideration. When information concerning different resources—such as wildlife, minerals, plants, hydrology (water), and soils—is entered into GIS, managers can look across disciplines and see the big picture. For example, the habitats of endangered species can be seen along with standard hydrology and vegetation maps.

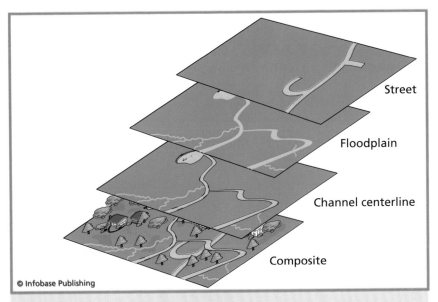

Street

Floodplain

Channel centerline

Composite

© Infobase Publishing

A Geographic Information System (GIS) can integrate several layers of data, called themes, and allow a land manager to model impacts to wildlife habitat.

GIS technology is used by resource managers for a number of purposes such as determining the suitability of an area for wildlife habitat, mapping areas at risk for fire, or assessing the health of rangelands and riparian areas in order to manage the health of wildlife.

Another advantage of GIS is its ability to show changes over time. By comparing old data with new data for the same location, it is possible to see which areas have changed and have been impacted the most. Trends can also be projected into the future. In Southern California, support for managing commercial development in San Diego and Los Angeles to protect rare desert species was boosted when the public was able to see—through GIS modeling—projected results of development trends over time. This resulted in the protection of more than 81,000 hectares (200,070 acres) of desert habitat.

As GIS technologies become more accessible, land managers increasingly use GIS to make decisions and communicate with the public. GIS allows people to see data at both large and small scales. This information allows scientists to create models that will show effects of different actions over time, illustrate long-term trends, and predict future conditions. To many, GIS technology alone has made possible the change in the way natural resource decisions are made.

Providing for White-Tailed Deer Habitat Using GIS

When a geographer or biologist wants to model white-tailed deer habitat using Geographic Information System (GIS), they must consider the following variables:

- What kinds of food do white-tailed deer eat?
- Is there adequate cover for shelter, such as trees or caves?
- Is there a reliable water source nearby?
- Is there enough open space to move around in?

A GIS analyst would use the above information to locate, based on the themes (food, cover, water, or space), possible deer habitat locations. For example, riparian areas (areas associated with streams) are prime deer habitat because they generally have better plant diversity, better soil moisture, better fertility, and a greater abundance of food.

Once these areas have been identified, the GIS specialist would look for the areas that best cover these first four criteria. Other information can also be used to refine the selected area. For example, layers can be added for elevation of the land, the terrain type (valley, mountain), or the slope and aspect of the land. (Sometimes vegetation that deer eat only grows on one side of the mountain—such as the north side.) In this case, north-facing slopes can be added into the model. Other components that can be added that affect deer habitat are the presence of roads (deer try to avoid roads), the amount of peace and solitude in the area (which deer prefer), or the presence of both summer and winter range. (Deer move down to lower elevations in the winter because food at higher elevations can be scarce, requiring them to migrate.)

When all the significant criteria important for deer habitat in a specific area have been identified and mapped, the areas that best meet all the criteria are where deer habitat would be modeled as to likely exist.

Before wildlife habitat sites can be planned for and protected, the areas need to be identified. An effective and highly advanced approach to this with GIS is called habitat modeling. In order to create a working model, scientists and land managers must identify all the factors involved, such as food availability, vegetation cover, forest type, topography, water resources, distance from urban areas, presence of roads, elevation of the land, and slope of the mountains.

Once this data is collected and digitally entered into a GIS system, the resulting model can identify the most suitable habitats. Data—such as soil types—can be digitized from existing soil survey maps, satellite imagery can be used, and data can be collected in the field using Global Positioning System (GPS). It can then be entered as layers into the GIS model and used to create habitat maps. Using a combination of data layers, a skilled GIS analyst can identify both areas of likely habitat and areas not compatible with the specific wildlife being studied.

Maps and products associated with these efforts assist natural resource biologists, watershed scientists, county planners, policy makers, and concerned citizens by providing consistent information. The information helps decision makers at both regional and local levels to answer questions, produce products, and provide information, including developing and depicting a broad range of conservation strategies for fish and wildlife habitats.

From wild game to endangered species, it is becoming increasingly more difficult to monitor and manage wildlife over a wide area without the use of GIS. Many different types of models can be created using different combinations of the data layers. Which model is created is determined by which questions conservationists and land managers need to have answers for. Some of the most common models used include vegetation, fire, habitat, watershed, and treatment modeling.

By modeling vegetation types, scientists can gather a lot of information about wildlife habitat. When vegetation exists in an area that a specific species likes, those areas are more likely to be that animal's natural habitat instead of an area that does not have the type of food it prefers. Vegetation information is always an important layer in modeling wildlife habitat because vegetation is important for not only food, but also shelter and protection.

Fire modeling analyzes the ability of vegetation to burn. During wildfires, many components affect the way a fire can be predicted to behave, such as humidity, wind speed and direction, and type of vegetation and its dryness. Fire modeling is important for wildlife habitat so that managers can predict which areas are safest for wildlife.

Habitat modeling is done to predict wildlife species distribution across landscapes. Models can predict the presence or absence of a species, its range, and the populations of species at different locations. Each model—and the layers used in GIS—are specific to the species being studied. The species' distribution and density measurement is used by wildlife biologists to determine how healthy the ecosystem and its biodiversity are. Habitat modeling is critical when threatened and endangered species are being studied. Habitat can be modeled for an abundance of species, such as bears, wolves, moose, birds, antelope, elk, and deer.

Watershed modeling is used to study, predict, and control erosion of the land after fires, sedimentation, and flooding and the impacts to wildlife. Treatment modeling is used to monitor the land and attempt to manage wildfires. For areas that are overgrown, a prescribed treatment may involve thinning the natural vegetation or conducting a prescribed burn (burning small areas intentionally to clear dead biomass out and reduce the amount of fuel available to burn). Models can also be used during restoration after a wildfire when areas are being managed by reseeding. Reseeding is a conservation measure that helps keep invasive species from outcompeting native species and taking over their habitat. It also provides for wildlife habitat, food sources, and protection.

These GIS models are powerful tools that enable scientists, conservationists, land managers, and the public to work productively together to better manage and provide for wildlife and their ecosystems.

USES OF ANIMALS

The relationship between humans and animals is as old as human history, going back thousands of years to the time when wild animals were drawn to the campfires of humans. Over time, animals and humans began to trust, and rely on, each other. Humans provided animals with shelter, food, and protection from predators. Animals, in turn, provided humans with food, clothing, and companionship. The meat of animals provided nutrients essential for survival, and animal skins provided warmth and shelter from the elements.

People cherish their animal companions for their unconditional affection and acceptance. People are easily awed when they observe wildlife in nature, such as buffalo, deer, elk, moose, bears, eagles, hawks, and many other species. In the United States during the early 1900s, most Americans lived on farms and had daily exposure to all types of animals, such as cows, sheep, horses, pigs, and chickens. Today, only 2% to 3% of the population still lives on farms. The rest—who live in urban areas—have come to rely on other animals in their lives, such as cats, dogs, birds, fish, and **exotic** pets. This chapter explores the multitude of important uses for animals, milestones in history regarding animals that have changed and improved our lives, and ways to get involved with animals.

THE ADVANCEMENT OF CIVILIZATION

One of the first major uses of animals that impacted the lives of humans was domestication. Early humans realized that when animals were domesticated, they could assist in plowing. In the Middle East and Turkey, farmers began raising sheep and goats. In Southeast Asia, they began to raise pigs and chickens. Originally, around 3,500 B.C., oxen were used to pull primitive plows. Later on, in Europe, the horseshoe and horse collar were invented, and over time, many farmers changed to heavy horses—such as draft horses—which could move faster than oxen. Today, in the United States, very few farmers actually use animals to help with plowing their fields, but farmers in the third world countries still rely heavily on animals.

In the Middle East, animals provide an important means of transportation for nomadic tribes. These people can travel across an inhospitable desert environment for several days on camels.

Animals have played a crucial role in American history, as well. For example, during the great expansion westward in the 1800s, oxen and horses had a significant role in pulling covered wagons and supplies across the country. After western expansion began, horses were used in the Pony Express to deliver mail to remote locations. Horse-drawn carriages provided transportation for much of the country. Miners working in remote mountain sites used burros to haul equipment and supplies. In South America, people use llamas and alpacas to carry camping gear and other equipment.

PRODUCTS FROM ANIMALS

Many products are derived from animals. As lifestyles have moved from farming, people often forget the importance animals play in our lives every day. For example, much of our food comes from animals—such

Alpacas, like llamas, are native to South America but are becoming more popular in the United States. These members of the Camelid family are very gentle. Their wool produces high quality products, such as sweaters. *(a, Photo by Nature's Images; b, Courtesy of Blue Moon Ranch in Woodland, Utah [www.bluemoonranch.com])*

as meat products, pet food, dairy products (ice cream, butter, cheese, and milk), and eggs. We also obtain other products from animals, such as wool for clothing, rugs, and blankets. Leather for shoes, furniture, belts, sports equipment, drum heads, luggage, and chamois cleaning cloths come from animals, as does **down** for pillows and comforters. We also obtain natural bristle brushes and toiletries and cosmetics that contain animal products, such as mink oil and lanolin, from animals.

Increasing in popularity in the United States is raising llamas and alpacas for their fine, long wool, which is used in clothing and blankets. Some people raise bees, which are needed to pollinate flowers so that fruit can grow, and which also make honey.

AGRICULTURE

Most farmers take seriously their role as stewards and work hard to do the best job possible of animal care, land management, and conservation. Their hard work and more efficient production systems have helped keep United States food prices among the lowest in the world.

Many producers of livestock—such as beef, poultry, and pork—have adopted voluntary animal care guidelines to make sure that animals are treated humanely. Their practices are based on veterinary science principles as well as technical knowledge gained from practical experience. These stewards of livestock have a commitment to the animal's health and welfare. Their practices include humane handling, good quality food and water, safe housing, disease prevention, veterinary care, and humane transportation. Many producers of livestock also finance and support ongoing research concerning the animal's welfare, such as implementing new diet guidelines, controlling disease, and providing for the animal's habitat.

BIOMEDICAL RESEARCH

Animals have contributed immensely in biomedical research. They have played a key role in the development of treatments for many diseases—both human and nonhuman. Many different types of animals are used in research, such as mice and rabbits. These animals are used because their genome is similar to the human genome. By applying treatments and observing an animal's response, many life-saving medications have been developed, increasing our quality of life.

According to C. Everett Koop, the former U.S. surgeon general, "Virtually every major medical advance for both humans and animals has been achieved through biomedical research by using animal models to study and find a cure for disease, and through animal testing to provide the safety and efficiency of a new treatment. Without the use of animals in research, continued medical milestones will be stifled." Biomedical research is covered more thoroughly in Chapter 6.

ANIMALS IN NATURE

Animals and nature go hand in hand. They are a key element of the natural world. Many people center their activities on wildlife. For example, bird-watching enthusiasts can spend hours hiking in areas that support a wide range of bird habitat. One of the most popular attractions to some of the national parks in the United States is the opportunity to see wildlife, such as the black bears, moose, wolves, and buffalo that are often seen at Yellowstone National Park.

Humans play a large role in maintaining the health of wildlife in nature. A well-balanced wildlife resource is healthy, productive, and in balance with the surrounding environment. Some people that are employed by the United States government are wildlife managers. It is their job to work toward maintaining the greatest possible numbers and varieties of wildlife on a continuing basis.

Because humans have such a tremendous impact on the environment, it is up to them to act responsibly, manage natural resources wisely, and develop policies that assure the continued availability of wildlife resources for future generations—a concept referred to as *sustainable use*.

Without effective management techniques, the right balance may not be maintained for all species, and some species could become threatened or endangered. Humans can impact the natural balance of wildlife by destroying habitat that is important to the biodiversity of the area, such as removing natural areas and building cities in their place. Pollution from human activities—including land, air, and water pollution—can threaten the health and well-being of wildlife. Overhunting and illegally hunting (poaching) certain animal species is another factor that can endanger the wildlife in nature and upset the balance. This is why there are specific restrictions and rules that hunters must obey. If hunters eliminate too many of a species, it can threaten the species' existence, or if hunters eliminate females—such as female deer—it can threaten the reproductivity of a species in a habitat, which in turn causes the effects to ripple across many interrelated components in the system.

Federal laws have been enacted making it illegal to hunt and kill endangered or threatened species. Similar laws have been put in place internationally to prohibit the sale of animal products from endangered species. Wildlife biologists have a challenging job maintaining and conserving natural habitat with all the other land use demands being placed on the land today.

ANIMALS AT HOME AND WORK

Some social scientists speculate that people in modern societies keep pets because they feel cut off from nature. Today, many people live in urban areas—such as in cities—where there are not many animals. When people care for pets, they provide them with three very important things: shelter, food, and affection.

Most Americans claim to be animal lovers. According to the American Pet Products Manufacturers Association, 62% of American households own at least one pet, and 47% own more than one. In addition, surveys have determined that the overwhelming majority of pet owners think of their pets as "friends." According to the Foundation for Animal Use Education, pet owners spend more than $30 billion each year on their cats, dogs, birds, fish, reptiles, rodents, and other small animals.

Pets make our lives more worthwhile. They provide friendship and companionship. They give us something to care for. However, despite the universal human need to feel close to animals, the bond of trust between pets and humans is often broken. Many people mistreat animals, either out of anger or ignorance. The most common types of animal abuse are neglect and abandonment. Many people who buy pets grow bored when the animals grow up. Some pet owners don't take the time to train their pets properly and then blame the animal for not being housebroken. Unwanted pets are often turned loose on the streets. As a result, animal shelters are filled with millions of unwanted pets.

Today, pet overpopulation is an important issue for communities to address. Many pets end up at local shelters because their owners cannot care for them. This is one reason experts advise pet owners to be responsible and spay or neuter their pets.

Some animals have jobs. Since the domestication of animals, humans have depended on dogs, horses, and other animals to assist with work and provide services. For example, urban police departments are using mounted patrols on horses to increase the presence of law enforcement in parks and pathways where cars cannot easily go.

As we will see in the next chapter, both dogs and horses provide many valuable services to society every day.

ANIMALS IN EDUCATION

Animals play an important role in the education of people of all ages. Each year, more than 135 million people visit zoos and aquariums in the United States. More than 9 million students are able to take school field trips to these places every year. These programs have become very popular over the years because of the increasing interest people have shown toward animals and learning about their environments. These programs not only present a wonderful way for experts to teach students about a particular species (often with the hands-on experience of seeing or touching the animal being presented), but they also provide an excellent opportunity to teach about the issues of conservation and the Earth's biodiversity.

These programs have begun in countries all over the world. Wildlife experts believe zoos and aquariums are a key component in stimulating public interest in threatened or endangered species—such as dolphins, tigers, elephants, and many species of birds. Through their exposure to these animals and the hands-on experiences they have with them, millions of people around the world have learned the importance of supporting international policies to conserve these animals. Also, the knowledge gained by those experts who handle, work with, and observe these animals in captivity have been vital in bringing some species back from near-extinction.

Animals can also teach us about specific aspects of behavior, such as love and compassion. Pets, such as dogs, are often faithful and loving toward their owners—hence the creation of a phrase heard often: "Dog is man's best friend." But animals also show love and allegiance to each other. For example, cats and dogs that grow up in the same house often treat each other as siblings rather than different species. It is common for cats and dogs in the same family to protect each other.

Scientists have been able to learn a lot about animal behavior from other types of animals, as well. One of the best-known examples is

Koko, a lowland gorilla. Koko, cared for and studied at a facility, has been able to learn sign language from a group of scientists. She asked for a pet one day, and the scientists gave her a kitten of her own. Koko lovingly cared for the kitten. In fact, Koko showed many of the same feelings for the kitten that people show toward their pets.

ANIMALS IN ENTERTAINMENT

Animals also provide people with an important form of entertainment, as evidenced by the popularity of movies or television programs such as *Mr. Ed, Lassie, The Bear, Gentle Ben, Black Beauty, Thomasina, Free Willy, The Black Stallion, Sea Biscuit, 101 Dalmatians, Paulie,* and *Homeward Bound*—to name a few. Animals in movies have a way of captivating us and igniting our imaginations. People can love, laugh, and relate to the antics and experiences of animals. Each time a new animal star appears on-screen, it helps people to bond with and appreciate that animal more. Just as learning more about endangered species helps people to understand them better and want to protect them, learning about animals in movies has the same effect.

Thoroughbred horse racing is a popular animal sport. Racehorses are capable of speeds up to 40 miles (64 km) per hour. Horse owners and track operators work together to develop policies to make sure the horses are being cared for properly. State regulators oversee the handling of racehorses through racing commissions.

The modern horse industry includes not only horse racing, but showing and recreation as well. Through instruction at equestrian facilities, many people have learned to ride and jump horses, not only for show but also as a popular form of recreation.

Rodeos are among America's most popular spectator sports. According to the Professional Rodeo Cowboys Association (PRCA)—the nation's largest and oldest professional rodeo organization—the national rodeo circuit includes about 700 PRCA-sanctioned events every year. Contestants compete for more than $28 million in prizes.

The PRCA has a rigorous program to make sure rodeo animals are treated humanely. Veterinarians specializing in equine (horse) and

Animals play a major role in many types of sports and recreation, such as equestrian sports. *(Julie A. Kerr, Nature's Images)*

bovine (cow) health have provided technical assistance in the development of specific rules for the humane treatment of the animals. A veterinarian is on site at every PRCA rodeo to monitor animal health and safety and to treat injuries when they occur. Although rodeo events can be physically challenging, injury rates for the animals are low.

The circus is another important event that people can attend to learn about animals and their behavior. They teach us how humans and animals interact. The animal training techniques used in circuses involve a system of reward and repetition that builds mutual respect and reinforces the trust between animal and trainer. These same techniques are what pet owners use to train their own pets to repeat certain behaviors, such as training a dog to catch a ball or Frisbee or teaching a parrot to talk.

Circus animals receive around-the-clock care from veterinarians and animal-handling professionals. The constant contact and daily nurturing foster trust and affection between the animals and their human caretakers. The resulting bond creates a remarkable partnership that is visible in the amazing circus performances the audience sees. Training methods are based on positive reinforcement in the form of food rewards and words of praise.

The U.S. Department of Agriculture (USDA) regularly reviews circus-animal care practices. The USDA can even conduct surprise inspections to make sure the animals are being cared for properly and responsibly by the circuses. Circuses also play an active role in wildlife conservation. Several circus organizations have established nonprofit organizations to provide financial support for various species, such as the African and Asian elephants. These organizations have developed many programs, including research programs, antipoaching programs, and reproduction research.

ANIMALS IN RECREATION

Many forms of recreation include animals. Many people take their dogs to the park, where they spend hours teaching their pet to catch a Frisbee or retrieve a ball. Many hikers and backpackers take their dogs with them while they're in the wilderness. Dogs not only provide companionship, but because they have such a keen sense of smell, they also provide a service of security because they can often detect the presence of other animals—such as moose—before their owners can.

Many people ride packhorses when they camp in the wilderness. In areas that are not accessible by cars, horses are often used to help carry camping gear, food, water, clothes, and other supplies.

Equestrian facilities—riding schools—are also a very popular form of recreation. Children and adults can learn about horses and how to care for them as well as gain skills in leisure riding, dressage, or show jumping. Equestrian facilities also teach about the interaction, bonds, and trust that must exist between a horse and rider in order to have a memorable partnership.

Another recreational activity that is gaining in popularity in the northern states is sled-dog racing. The most famous sled-dog race, which is held every year in Alaska, is called the Iditarod. Many refer to it as the "Last Great Race on Earth" because it requires—of both people and dogs—a hardworking, individualistic, survive-against-the-odds pioneering attitude.

The Iditarod sled-dog race is an Alaskan tradition that has gained in popularity over the past 30 years. Each year, in March, thousands of excited sled dogs line up in downtown Anchorage, eager to begin their marathon journey to Nome—about 1,100 miles (1,770 km) away. This race is one of the most unique and rigorous athletic tests there is.

The Iditarod pits both men and women (called mushers) and their dogs against raging blizzards, rugged mountain terrain, and bitter Arctic

A Celebration of Life—What the Iditarod Really Represents

The Iditarod was inspired by a monumental and historic event—a sled-dog relay of life-saving serum from Anchorage to Nome in 1925. That January, in the middle of a bitterly cold winter, a deadly disease called diphtheria broke out in the small town of Nome, Alaska, near the Bering Sea. The nearest serum to fight diphtheria was in Anchorage, Alaska—almost 1,000 miles (1,609 km) away with nothing but Alaskan wilderness in between.

The Alaska Railroad carried the medicine 250 miles (418 km) north to Nenana. From there, 20 volunteer sled-dog drivers (or *mushers*) relayed the serum nonstop the remaining 674 miles (1,085 km). When the first musher left Nenana, the temperature hovered at −50°F (−46°C). According to the legend, the serum was nearly lost when a huge gust of wind toppled the sled of the final musher. The musher frantically dug the serum out of the snow with his bare hands, righted his sled, and continued on. Through the efforts of those heroic mushers and dogs, the serum was finally delivered to Nome five days and seven hours after leaving Nenana. The sled dogs helped save the people of Nome.

cold as they travel over frozen rivers and historic trails in a spectacular wilderness setting. Mushers develop a special bond with their traveling companions—their dogs. The dogs, who are lean and fast, love to run. Today, Iditarod mushers brave much of the same wild Alaskan trail that the early heroes traveled to deliver the life-saving serum for diphtheria to Nome. The dogs are well-trained and obedient to their mushers. Dogs and mushers have a strong, mutually respectful bond. The mushers even train in the summer by harnessing the dog team to a cart on wheels. An Iditarod team is a beautiful example of the natural bonds that can be achieved between people and animals.

THE 4-H CLUB

The 4-H Club is a national club established to help people improve their lives and learn many different types of skills, such as sewing, cooking, computer technology, and other community-improvement skills. Many of their activities are centered around animals. For example, they provide members with opportunities to train, groom, and show their dogs. They sponsor equestrian activities such as training, grooming, and showing horses. There are also activities to teach about the care and welfare of farm animals, such as sheep, goats, and cattle and opportunities to demonstrate those skills at county and state fairs.

THE HUMANE SOCIETY OF THE UNITED STATES

The Humane Society of the United States is an organization formed in 1954 that strives to make a difference in the lives of animals in the United States and around the world. It is dedicated to creating a world where people's relationships with animals are guided by compassion. The Humane Society strives to educate people to respect animals for their intrinsic value. They also look out for the welfare of the animal in an attempt to ensure that animals are not exploited and harmed in research, laboratory tests, or kept in deplorable conditions on farms.

The Humane Society provides many services in their quest to protect animals from abuse and exploitation. Its members work with pet owners, teaching the basic concepts of proper animal care; they participate in wildlife and habitat protection; and they have a marine mammal program to help ensure proper handling of whales, manatees, and other marine mammals both in the wild and in captivity. They participate in politics at federal, state, and local levels to obtain better conditions for animals. They are also involved in farm animal welfare activities to promote more humane treatment of animals in the meat, egg, and milk industries.

They conduct animal research campaigns to raise awareness of pain and distress suffered by animals. They investigate reports of animal mistreatment, and they also work with animal shelters that adopt pets to qualified owners. Some psychologists believe that when people are kind to animals and show them respect, it is an important reflection on the way they approach the world in both attitude and behavior.

THE IMPORTANCE OF ANIMALS

This chapter looks at some of the reasons animals are important to us—it identifies many of the diverse goods and services that animals provide in people's lives every day. It outlines the importance of animals in medical research and how they have improved the quality of life for many people and have extended people's life expectancies. It looks at ecotourism and the role of America's national parks, wildlife preserves, and refuges. Next, it explores the ways that people depend on animals for the services they provide. It discusses beneficial insects and their role in biological pest control. It looks at exotic pets and why they are so fascinating to so many people. Finally, it addresses animal intelligence and what people can learn from animals, as well as career options involving wildlife.

MEDICAL RESOURCES

Throughout history, scientists have been solving medical problems, developing new techniques and treatments, and curing diseases by using animals in biomedical research. Animals have played a major role in medical research for both humans and animals. They have contributed to the creation of vaccines, cancer therapies, life-saving surgical procedures, the development of safe consumer products, and organ transplantation. There is a relationship between biomedical research and medical progress. Animals have contributed greatly since the late 1800s in discovering cures for many serious diseases.

Animals are used in research because their organs and body systems are similar to humans, and oftentimes, they are susceptible to the same diseases as humans. When experimenting in a laboratory setting, it is much easier for scientists to control the environment—if the environment wasn't controlled, other outside factors could interfere, and scientists might never find a cure to the disease being studied. Also, because an animal's life span is relatively short compared to humans, it allows researchers to study them throughout their entire lives.

Laboratory mice are used in research more often than any other animal species. Mice and other rodents—such as hamsters and rats—account for more than 90% of the animals used in research. Other animal species, such as dogs, cats, farm animals, rabbits, frogs, fish, monkeys, and birds account for the other 10%.

Animals are used in research after scientists have completed computer model simulations and cell or tissue culture research. With the knowledge gained through research on animals, researchers believe they can continue improving the lives of not only humans, but also our pets, wildlife, and other animals. The table on page 94 lists some of the medical advances made possible through the contributions of specific animals.

Animal research that has benefited animals directly includes vaccines for feline leukemia, **rabies**, parvovirus, and distemper, as well as treatments for cancer, hip dysplasia, and heartworm disease. Animal research has also benefited many endangered species. Through the knowledge and technical methods developed by means of animal research, scientists have not only been able to preserve species, but enable them to reproduce and increase in number.

Animal care is regulated in research labs by the U.S. Department of Agriculture under the federal Animal Welfare Act. The National Institutes of Health also administers guidelines for the care and use of animals in laboratories. When academic institutions use animals in their research, they must follow the federal rules as well as local animal care and use committee guidelines.

Medical Advancements Made Possible Through Animal Research

Contribution	Animal Used
Rabies treatment	Dogs
Anthrax treatment	Sheep
Modern anesthesia	Dogs
Rheumatoid arthritis	Rabbits, monkeys
Antibiotic development	Rats, mice, rabbits
Polio prevention	Rabbits, monkeys, rodents
Measles and rubella prevention	Monkeys
Gene therapy for cystic fibrosis	Mice, primates
Smallpox treatment	Cows
Discovery of insulin	Dogs
Tetanus prevention	Horses
Diphtheria prevention	Horses
Whooping cough treatment	Guinea pigs, rabbits
Chemotherapy development (for cancer)	Monkeys, rabbits
Advances in cardiology	Dogs
Genetic heart disorders research	Mice

(Source: Foundation for Animal Use Education)

While many people support the use of animals in biomedical research, some are strongly opposed to it. They do not believe animals should be put in any compromised position, such as lab research, school dissections, or in product testing to ensure certain manufactured products are safe for human use. They recommend instead that computer models be used for research rather than using a live animal. Many scientists agree that while a certain amount of animal research can be done this way, animal research is still critical to the future of medical advances. This remains a heated issue between the opposing sides.

ECOTOURISM AND AMERICA'S NATIONAL PARKS, WILDLIFE PRESERVES, AND REFUGES

Ecotourism is a huge industry in the United States. Many people enjoy summer vacations that consist of outdoor and wilderness experiences that include camping, backpacking, fishing, hiking, canoeing, kayaking, and wildlife observation. According to the National and State Economic Impacts of Wildlife Watching Addendum, 66 million Americans spend more than $38 billion each year on outdoor activities that involve observing, feeding, or photographing wildlife.

In order to protect these valuable wildlife resources, the U.S. National Park Service has designated unique areas across the country to be preserved and protected as national parks, wildlife preserves, and wildlife refuges. In many areas, national parks and refuges represent the last remaining areas of once vast, undisturbed ecosystems. These areas also serve as outdoor laboratories for the study of physical, biological, and cultural systems and their components. The Park Service's mission is to manage biological resources and related ecosystem processes.

The National Park Service has been a leader in the global national park movement. The world's first national park—Yellowstone—was established by the Congress in 1872. Since then, the idea of creating nationally significant parks has spread to more than 100 countries. The National Park Service also provides technical assistance and advice to countries around the globe.

National Parks provide visitors with opportunities to view rarely seen wildlife. The moose (a) and bear (b) are two species that can be seen at Yellowstone National Park. *(Courtesy of the U.S. Fish and Wildlife Service)*

More than 280 million recreational visitors visit America's national parks each year. According to the Travel Industry Association of America, visiting national parks is the second most popular vacation activity of American travelers. According to the World Tourism Organization, nature-related tourism accounts for over 20% of all international travel.

Participating in nature-related activities also has aesthetic (something pleasing to the senses) and spiritual benefits. Many people find nature soothing and rejuvenating. Many believe that the benefits from being among wildlife are priceless.

SERVICES PROVIDED BY ANIMALS— MAKING OUR LIVES BETTER

Some animals—such as dogs and horses—are extremely valuable for the services they provide to humans. In fact, many peoples' lives depend on the critical services performed by these dedicated, noble animals.

Therapeutic Horseback Riding

Several areas in the United States have opened therapeutic riding facilities. Therapeutic horseback riding programs bring remarkable benefits that improve the quality of life for those with disabilities, often giving them a chance to participate in an activity that not only helps them physically, but emotionally as well, by engaging them in a rewarding activity and a unique form of independence. Therapeutic riding centers provide a safe and secure environment not only for the physically handicapped, but also for youth at risk and victims of domestic violence. The sense of empowerment and security generated from riding these horses is another example of an important aesthetic benefit that animals have to offer. Participants in these programs experience an increase in balance, strength, muscle tone, self-confidence, and social awareness.

Guide Dogs for the Blind

Dogs are often referred to as "Man's Best Friend." Perhaps this is because of the valuable roles they play in peoples' lives. Some dogs are trained to assist those people who cannot see. These dogs—called guide dogs—are trained professionals. Their skills are developed to enable them to perform their job with confidence. They differ from pet dogs in that they have been carefully bred, raised, and trained for the sole purpose of providing a safe means of mobility for people who are blind or visually impaired. They must be intelligent, alert, and willing to serve. Purebred labrador retrievers, German shepherds, golden retrievers, and labrador/golden retriever crosses are the breeds most commonly used as guide dogs.

Training for these extraordinary dogs begins when they are just six to eight weeks old. Volunteer puppy walkers introduce the pups to the sights, smells, and sounds of the world in which they will play such an important part. They are taken on buses and trains, into shops, and along busy streets.

When they are a year old, they begin their formal training. They are taught the skills needed to guide a blind or partially sighted person. For example, they learn to walk in a straight line in the center of the sidewalk, unless there is an obstacle in the way; they learn not to turn corners unless told to do so; they stop at curbs and wait for the command to cross the road, or to turn left or right; they are taught to judge height and width so that their owner does not bump his or her head or shoulder; and they are taught how to deal with traffic.

The training they go through is very strict and demanding—and not all dogs pass their training. Although their training is highly specialized, the same basic principles of consistency, repetition, and praise are applied as they are in all successful animal training. For those that pass, they are then coached with the person they will be assisting, and that partnership becomes a strong, mutual bond. They become a loving companion. Most guide dogs work about seven years. For the visually impaired owner, this could be the first time they have been independent for a long time. A guide dog's work is incredibly demanding, and their owner's safety depends on the dog's concentration. Once a guide dog is retired, it is adopted out to a loving family.

Hearing Dogs for the Deaf

Hearing dogs assist deaf and hard-of-hearing individuals by nudging or pawing their partners to get them to respond to a variety of household sounds such as a door knock or doorbell, alarm clock, oven buzzer, kitchen timer, telephone, baby cry, name call, or smoke alarm. These dogs are trained to lead their deaf partners to the source of the sound.

Hearing dogs are generally mixed breeds acquired from animal shelters and are small to medium in size. Personality and temperament are important for a hearing dog. They must be energetic and ready to work in an instant when a sound occurs. They must also be friendly and people oriented. The most commonly used breeds include terrier mixes, poodles, cocker spaniels, Lhasa apsos, shih tzus, and Chihuahuas. Most of these dogs are between eighteen months to two years old. It usually takes about six months to train these dogs. Before they begin their official training, these dogs are raised and socialized by volunteer puppy raisers. Hearing dogs are identified by an orange collar or vest. Hearing dogs increase the owner's feelings of security and confidence.

Support Dogs

These service dogs—also called assistance dogs—are trained to serve those who need assistance with various mobility tasks. They are trained to open doors, retrieve small and distant objects, carry bags, rise to counters, and pull those in wheelchairs. They also provide constant companionship and emotional support to the person they are placed with. Assistance dogs are often labrador and golden retrievers and begin their training once they are about three months old.

Assistance dogs can be trained to specifically meet the owner's needs. They can be street-certified, which means they can accompany their person in all situations. They are referred to as *para* or *quad* dogs. Para dogs have the strength and physical structure to pull a wheelchair up steep embankments. Quad dogs usually accompany their person, who is in an electric wheelchair.

Home-certified dogs are trained to only work indoors. Home companion dogs are dogs trained mainly for companionship, but they do have minimal retrieval skills. These types of service dogs are used often for elderly care and for those who are bedridden or who cannot leave home. Many studies concerning elderly companionship have shown that life expectancy increases for those elderly who have close relationships with companion animals.

Social and Facility Dogs

Animal-assisted therapy programs also use support dogs. It has been shown that there is a correlation between recovery times for hospital patients and animal interaction. Some programs provide opportunities for dogs and their owners to visit hospitals, nursing homes, rehabilitation centers, psychiatric wards, and various other healthcare facilities. These dogs are not breed specific, but must have a loving, gentle temperament and a willingness to be touched. They are taught obedience skills, as well as how to work around various kinds of hospital equipment and a variety of patient conditions.

Search and Rescue Dogs

Some dogs are used exclusively to assist in search and rescue operations. These dogs are as specialized as any dog can be. The use of dogs for search and rescue is not new. Specially trained dogs have been used around the world for decades. These dogs have been successful in searching for victims trapped in rubble created by earthquakes, tornadoes, mudslides, flooding, avalanches, or explosions; Alzheimer's patients who have wandered away; children, hunters, campers, the elderly, or mentally disabled who have become lost; and victims of boating accidents.

They work hard to find and rescue people who are trapped or lost. They are able to do this because they have a keen sense of smell. These dogs can often mean the difference between life and death. They have been used to help solve kidnappings and find lost hikers in rugged mountain situations. By smelling something of the victim's—such as clothing or other personal objects—they can track the path that the missing person took. They played a critical role in the search and rescue operations associated with the terrorist attacks in the United States that took place on September 11, 2001.

Police Patrol Dogs

Police patrol dogs are trained and used in many types of situations. These dogs assist police officers in locating evidence, such as shell casings, guns, and knives. They are able to find dead bodies to help solve crimes. They are trained to locate surface remains and makeshift graves, or to find objects in landfills. They also accompany officers on patrol and can assist on immobilizing criminals so that they can't escape the police. They have been instrumental in solving many difficult crimes.

Bomb Detection Dogs

Some police dogs are trained to specialize in the detection of bombs and other explosive devices. When a security team is faced with bomb detection, the "bomb sniffing dog" is often the most important field asset for a mission's success and the officer's survival. These dogs not only provide a valuable service to police forces around the world, but also to military units.

Narcotic Detection Dogs

Narcotic dogs—or drug dogs—are specially trained dogs used for drug search and detection in police K9 units. They learn a variety of skills and are able to adapt to many different environments and scenarios. They are used in operations from small drug stings to huge drug busts. These dogs not only detect and locate drugs, but also offer vital protection to the officer working with them.

Family Protection Dogs

Another important service that dogs provide is serving as a guard dog to protect families. Guard dogs are custom trained to fit the needs of the family (or business) that owns them. These dogs are extremely loyal and intelligent.

Regulatory Services

Dogs are also used extensively for services needed by the federal government. The U.S. Department of Agriculture (USDA) ensures the safety of animal and plant products that are imported and exported from the United States. The Animal and Plant Health Inspection Service (APHIS) is a department responsible for regulating the import and export of plants, animals, and agricultural products. Because of dogs' highly keen sense of smell, the federal government uses them to detect illegal materials being brought into, or moved through, the

This APHIS inspection dog is able to sniff out commodities being transported illegally. These dogs are well trained and are able to detect illegal drugs and illegally imported fruit and vegetables. *(Courtesy of the U.S. Department of Agriculture)*

United States. These include narcotics as well as certain types of produce such as fruits and vegetables. These highly specialized dogs are used in immigration offices and airports throughout the country.

BENEFICIAL INSECTS AND BIOLOGICAL PEST CONTROL

Over the past several decades, chemical pesticides have been widely used to fight exotic insects. Recently, however, because of increased environmental concern and safer alternatives, many farmers, gardeners, and home owners have switched to the use of "beneficial insects." Another reason for using beneficial insects to control pests is that

Many insects are beneficial to their native habitats. They can act as a natural form of pest control for agriculture and gardens. Two beneficial insects are the (a) praying mantis; and (b) the ladybug. *(a, courtesy of the U.S. Fish and Wildlife Service, by Gene Whitaker; b, courtesy of the U.S. Fish and Wildlife Service)*

targeted insects build up immunities over time to traditional chemical pesticides. Some farmers have begun combating this problem by planting genetically engineered crops that are more resistant to insect damage, as well as using the beneficial insects. These beneficial insects—or predator insects—help control the infestation and population of destructive species. Insect predators are already fully developed for a specific prey and are less likely to affect other aspects of the food chain. Natural predators are also longer lasting because insect prey does not quickly develop resistance to their predators, as they do with chemical insecticides. Today, roughly 300 predatory insects are currently used in 60 countries to control agricultural pests.

An important concept in gardening is called *companion planting*. In nature, a balanced system consists of thousands of different species of plants and animals working together. Some plants support beneficial insects. When these plants are used they provide a habitat for the beneficial insects that act as natural predators to insects that are destructive.

This concept is now gaining popularity for many gardeners. Companion planting is an example of the positive ways plants, insects, and their habitat can be used to keep pests away. In addition, a more diverse garden provides added habitat, shelter, and a food source (such as pollen and nectar) that many predators (beneficial insects) need in their diet.

The Unique Praying Mantis

A praying mantis (*Mantis religiosa*) is a carnivorous insect. Some can grow to six inches (15 cm) in length. The name *mantis* is a Greek word for *prophet* or *soothsayer*. The *Carolina mantis* is a common insect of the eastern United States. The European and Chinese mantises were introduced to the northeastern United States about 75 years ago as garden predators in the hopes of eliminating the pest insects.

Camouflage is very important for the praying mantis' survival. Because they have so many enemies—such as birds—they must be able to blend in with their habitat to avoid being eaten.

The Praying mantis is the only insect that can turn from side to side in a full 180° angle. Their eyes are sensitive to the slightest movement up to 60 feet (18 m) away. They have powerful jaws for devouring their prey. They have ultrasound ears, and their spiny front legs are held together in a praying position. The front legs are equipped with rows of sharp spines used to grasp its prey.

They wait, unmoving, and are almost invisible on a stem or leaf, ready to catch any insects that pass by. When potential prey comes close enough, the mantis thrusts its pincer-like forelegs forward to catch it. The prey cannot escape because the insect's forelegs are so strong and armed with overlapping spines. The mantis bites the neck of its prey to paralyze it, and then begins to devour it.

Praying mantises eat beetles, butterflies, spiders, crickets, and grasshoppers. They can also eat tree frogs, lizards, mice, and hummingbirds. Praying mantises are exceptional pest exterminators. They help control the populations of bugs that pose a threat to farming. These masters of disguise help farmers and gardeners.

Interestingly, this concept of natural pest management has been practiced since the dawn of agriculture. It has just been in recent decades that people have stopped practicing it because faster-acting, stronger chemicals—in the form of insecticides—have been developed and used. Over time, many of these companion planting techniques practiced by our ancestors were discarded—techniques developed from many years of trial and error and observation. For example, planting tomatoes next to carrots is beneficial in order to ward off the carrot fly.

Beneficial insects are also safe for the environment, plants, and people (unlike chemical insecticides). They can be used on many different types of plants and crops. They can be used in greenhouses, outdoor fields, indoors, under lights, and in home gardens. They eliminate the necessity of applying and reapplying chemicals. All the gardener has to do is plant the types of plants beneficial insects like along with the other plants in their gardens. Some of the most commonly used beneficial insects include the following:

- Ladybugs
- Praying mantises
- Caterpillar parasites

The Amazing Ladybug

Ladybugs—also called lady beetles—are great for keeping insect pests in control. A single adult ladybug can devour up to 60 aphids (a huge pest) a day. Ladybugs also feed on pollen and nectar in order to get through times when prey species are scarce. Some of the plants they are most attracted to are mint and catnip. They also like wild, native grasses and flowering weeds—such as golden rod and amaranth—to provide nectar as well as an area to stay in the winter. Hedgerows, windbreaks, and permanent plant borders give insects shelter from storms and bad weather. A shallow source of water allows them to reside in a particular habitat for an extended period of time.

- Fly parasites
- Green lacewings
- Mealy bug predators
- Pirate bugs
- Predatory mites
- Spider mite predators
- Thrips
- Whitefly parasites

The larvae of these tiny creatures are ravenous predators and parasites of many of the pest insects. Beneficial insects are also valuable because they pollinate crops and other plants. Of all the beneficial insects, the ladybugs, lacewings, and tiny pirate bugs are the most commonly encountered and likely to be the most easily attracted to plants in the garden.

The inclusion of very small flowers in the garden is the best way to attract and support beneficial insects—plants such as sunflowers, cone flowers, and chamomile. Chemical insecticides should not be used around beneficial insects because it kills them, as well as the pest insects.

The table on page 107 illustrates which predators can be used to control which pests and which plants can be used as the trap crop—a species of plant that acts as a lure for beneficial insects.

EXOTIC PETS

Humans share this planet with an incredible variety of animals. Even though there are thousands of species of animals, only a few have achieved the rank of what people consider as pets. There are many animals throughout history that people have tried to keep, train, and domesticate, such as lions, tigers, panthers, elephants, deer, bear, and moose. There are accounts throughout history of kings and emperors keeping exotic pets.

Many people today have rare and unusual pets, including such large snakes as boa constrictors, cobras, and pythons. People also keep skunks, raccoons, tarantulas, scorpions, llamas and alpacas, or miniature horses.

When people keep an animal that is not normally tamed or kept as a companion, it is called an "exotic" pet—a special or unusual pet.

Some scientists believe people are attracted to exotic pets because humans have a strong desire to tame wild creatures. Humans often find it especially rewarding to tame a creature from the wild and make it friendly.

THE AMAZING PARROT

Some of the most beautiful and rewarding exotic pets are parrots. One aspect about parrots that fascinates people is their ability to speak human words. Parrots are different from other birds because of the formation of their skull. Because their top beak is hinged on the front of their skull, and the bottom beak is connected to the skull by a ligament (a band of strong tissue that connects bones to each other), this makes their jaw similar to that of humans. They also have a short neck and a thick, fleshy tongue. Because of this, they can learn to speak human words.

Beneficial Insects Used to Control Unwanted Pests

Predator	Host pest	Associated companion plant
Lacewing	Aphids, thrips, mealy bug, caterpillars, mites	Caraway, dill, sunflowers, dandelion
Ground beetle	Slugs, snails, cutworm, cabbage maggot, small caterpillars	Sweet clover, mulches, groundcovers
Pirate bug	Thrips, spider mite, leafhopper, earworm, small caterpillars	Queen Anne's lace, strawberries, carrots, corn, daisies, coriander
Syrphid fly	Aphids	Dill, Queen Anne's lace, coriander, California lilac, sunflowers
Damsel bugs	Aphids, thrips, leafhopper, treehopper, small caterpillars	Sunflower, golden rod, alfalfa

All parrots have the capacity to speak, but not all will necessarily do so. A baby parrot will often learn words if it is spoken to, played with, and can listen to people interact with each other. Parrots learn by repetition and can learn to speak words of any language, although the vowel sounds are the easiest for them to say—which is why so many talking parrots can say "hello."

Parrots are fascinating creatures. Most experts believe that the African gray can speak the best—some of them have more than 200 words in their vocabulary. For parrots that are interacted with, and are willing to speak, it does not take long before they say "hello" when the phone rings or sound like they are blowing their nose when they see someone pick up a tissue. They are able to mimic many household sounds, such as dripping water from a faucet, a cuckoo clock, microwave beep, or a toilet flush.

Parrot Facts

- There are more than 300 species of parrots worldwide.
- Parrots can range in size from 8–36 inches (20–94 cm).
- African grays, lovebirds, and Indian ring-necked parakeets are found in Africa and Asia.
- Macaws and Amazon parrots are from South America.
- Cockatoos, cockatiels, and lories come from the South Pacific Islands and Australia.
- Conures come from the Caribbean Islands.
- Large parrots—like macaws—can live as long as 80 years.
- Small parrots can live 15 years or more.
- Parrots have an intelligence level similar to that of a three-year-old child.
- Like people, parrots try to attract attention by saying and doing things people respond to.
- Once someone has gained a parrot's trust, the parrot will try to please that person because it enjoys their company.

Many people find enjoyment in friendships with exotic pets such as parrots and miniature horses. (a) Parrots can be very loving, devoted pets. (b) Miniature horses are gentle, and many people use them to pull carts around yards. *(Julie A. Kerr, Nature's Images)*

One of the most rewarding aspects of having an exotic parrot that can speak, is that it is a true testament to the parrot's intelligence. Parrots not only teach us about the animal world, they also teach us about ourselves and our own capabilities.

LESSONS ABOUT LIFE—ANIMAL INTELLIGENCE

Observing and studying animals gives researchers insight into animal intelligence and helps us to understand characteristics unique to different species. It teaches us about social interactions and relationship dynamics. Animals and humans come closest in behavior that is based on instincts—the patterns that each species is born with. More complex animals, such as mammals, add learning, remembering, and thinking skills to these basic instincts. All of these skills combined can be studied and measured as a form of intelligence.

Many animals show strong characteristics of memory. For example, elephants on the African plains can migrate hundreds of miles in search of water and food. The older elephants seem to have a memory of where these places have been found in the past, and they can lead their troop there.

Pods of humpback whales migrate each year from the cold Arctic waters near Alaska in the summer to the warm tropical waters of Hawaii in the winter. This trip of several thousand miles (km) is repeated each year, and the time period of arrival and departure, as well as the route they travel, are consistent. The whales also communicate to each other on these amazing journeys through a series of clicks, hums, groans, and whistles that people commonly call whale song.

Humpback whales also exhibit planning and coordination in their hunting and trapping skills, which is also a useful measure of their intelligence and how their minds work. Humpbacks, up to 60 feet (18 m) long, feed on plankton—masses of tiny animals that float on the ocean's surface. In order to concentrate the plankton, one or two humpbacks will dive deep and spiral up toward the surface, releasing a stream of bubbles from their blowholes. This causes the bubbles to rise in a cylindrical curtain, drawing the plankton together into a central mass. The whales, by trapping them this way, can more effectively feed on that particular food source.

Whales are not the only species that demonstrates intelligence by migrating. Thousands of caribou walk from the northern slopes of Alaska to the forests of northern Alberta, Canada, and back each year. The calves that are born up in the northern reaches during the warm months are just big enough to be able to migrate south in the colder months.

Another amazing migratory animal is a bird called a turnstone. They spend their summers far north in Alaska, northern Canada, Scandinavia, and Siberia. In the winter, they migrate as far south as Australia, New Zealand, and South America.

People have also learned from watching animals. Some of the most important inventions come from the observation of specific animal characteristics. For instance, the first principles of flight that led to the discovery and advancement of airplanes were originally discovered through watching the movements of birds' wings during flight.

Whale Facts

- Whales can swim deep in the ocean, but they have to come up to the surface for air. Because of this, whales are mammals—they are not fish.
- The group of mammals called whales includes dolphins, porpoises, and whales. Some are gigantic, like the blue whale, which can grow to be as long as three school buses. Others are smaller. The harbor porpoise is about as long as a bicycle.
- Whales do not lay eggs like fish, but give birth to their babies.
- A newborn whale can already swim when it is born. They swim right to the surface for their first breath of air.
- Whales and dolphins find food by sending out sounds underwater that bounce onto other sea creatures and then bounce back. This is called echolocation. These sounds are so high pitched that humans cannot hear them. Echolocation is used to find food and to help whales navigate in the dark water.
- Whales have skin instead of scales like fish. Whales can live in very cold water because of their tough, spongy skin. The fat under their skin is called blubber and keeps them warm in cold water.
- Dolphins and whales travel in herds. As many as a thousand can travel together.
- Some whales sing songs that can be heard for miles and miles under the oceans. These songs are long and complex and give us some idea about the intelligence of whales.

Scientists were able to observe and study the process of **echolocation** from dolphins—dolphins can "see" or "sense" underwater by emitting a sonic beep and registering its return signal. Researchers discovered that dolphins were able to determine the size, distance, and direction of objects by measuring how long the animal's emitted signal took to strike the object and then return to the dolphin. Through the study of echolocation, researchers were able to develop the sonar that is used on submarines today.

JOBS INVOLVING WILDLIFE

Animals also provide many diverse employment opportunities. There are many jobs that exist today because of wildlife. Many people decide to have careers as wildlife biologists, animal care specialists, animal rescue and rehabilitation specialists, trainers, educators, and zookeepers.

Wildlife biologists can be involved in the study of many types of wildlife. They can record data in the wild through field work and direct observation. They can also track wild animals by radio. Radio telemetry is a tool used by scientists to gather information about animals they cannot observe directly. The animal to be studied must first be captured and fitted with a radio collar or a tiny implanted transmitter and then released. The transmitter emits radio pulses that can be picked up on a radio receiver. The distance and the direction of the signal can be tracked, which allows scientists to pinpoint the movements of the animal they are tracking. Scientists can also measure breathing rate and mating and social activity this way. Many wildlife biologists worldwide have gone into primitive jungle areas for years in order to observe different species, such as gorillas, in their natural habitat.

There are many diverse careers within the world of animal care, but they all focus on the care and protection of animals. These careers fall into two categories: working directly or indirectly with animals.

People who work directly with animals include veterinarians, pet groomers, and zookeepers. Zookeepers have an important role. The only opportunity some people have to see and learn about animals is by observing them in a zoo setting. People who work indirectly with animals include animal rights activists and those who work in pet stores.

Those who are involved in wildlife rescue work with many types of injured or abandoned animals in the wild, including hawks, eagles, raccoons, deer, owls, wolves, foxes, bears, turtles, swans, and squirrels, to name a few. These animals must be carefully nursed back to health, which can be a long process that takes several months of careful monitoring and care. Once animals are rehabilitated, they are released back into the wild. One of the most difficult aspects of the job for the caregiver is not knowing whether the animal survives after it is released, unless it is tracked.

Other professionals choose careers in animal-oriented education, as seen at facilities such as Sea World. Education works both ways. While trainers are able to teach the animals they care for, people are also learning—perhaps more than the animals themselves—about animal intelligence, response, behavior, and interactions.

People choose animal careers for many different reasons. One characteristic they all share, however, is a true love for animals. Some people enjoy training and teaching them—such as the trainers for seeing eye dogs. Some people desire to help animals in distress. Many want pets to be happy and healthy. People that live in the United States have more than 48 million dogs, 25 million cats, 23 million birds, 12 million exotic pets, and 340 million fish as pets—millions of good reasons to work in the world of animal care.

MANAGEMENT OF LAND, WATER, ANIMALS, AND ENVIRONMENT

Because many components make up a healthy, functioning ecosystem—animals, plants, soil, water, and air—all of the components must be addressed simultaneously in order to manage ecosystems effectively. Change in one component will have a ripple effect and impact the rest. For this reason, natural resource managers must perform a balancing act of sorts in order to account for the variability in a system and promote its overall health and survival.

This chapter looks at causes of endangerment—such as habitat destruction, introduction of exotic species, pollution, overexploitation, and habitat fragmentation. It addresses conservation planning and environmental impact analysis. It then examines difficult management issues such as the realities of poaching as well as the environmental devastation of oil spills from supertankers. Finally, it focuses on laws that have been put in place to protect endangered species.

CAUSES OF ENDANGERMENT

Endangerment is a broad issue that involves the habitats and environments where species live and interact with one another. This universal problem cannot be solved until humans protect the natural environments where the endangered species live.

Habitat Destruction

Our planet is continually changing, causing habitats to be altered and modified. The natural changes that occur on Earth usually happen at a gradual, slow pace. This type of change usually does not have a large impact on individual species. Unfortunately, when changes occur at a more rapid pace, there is little or no time for individual species to react and adjust to the new circumstances in their environment. The results can be disastrous. This is why rapid habitat loss is so serious.

Habitat destruction by humans—such as mining, logging, clearing trees for cattle grazing, building dams, constructing highways and cities—is the leading cause of species endangerment and extinction. Nearly every region on Earth has been affected by human activity—most notably in the past 100 years. For example, human activity has caused the extinction of fish and other aquatic species because of water pollution; humans have caused changes in global climate because of the release of greenhouse gasses into the atmosphere from cars and industry; and humans have destroyed the nutrients and structure of soil by cutting down forests and leaving bare ground in its place. It can take centuries to regrow a forest that was cut down by humans or destroyed by fire. Many of the world's threatened animals live in these forests. When their habitat is destroyed, the species that cannot adjust to the new conditions will die out and become extinct.

Introduction of Exotic Species

Animals that have existed in an area over time are called native species. They are well-adapted to their environment and have learned to survive and flourish with the other native species in the habitat. When exotic, or nonnative, species are introduced, however, they can threaten the native animals' existence. Nonnative species are often introduced by humans, either intentionally or accidentally. Some introduced species blend in naturally without causing a problem, but others can be very destructive by disrupting the delicate ecological balances.

Some introduced species put native species in danger by preying on them. This can alter the natural habitat and cause greater competition for food. Introduced species can completely wipe out native species. In fact, nearly 20% of known endangered vertebrates are threatened by introduced species. The introduced species may take over niches that other species traditionally occupied. They might also change the ecosystem enough to indirectly force out native species or bring in diseases to the environment that the native species are not immune to.

The effects of introduced species are most notable on islands. Introduced rats, pigs, cats, and other species have caused the endangerment and extinction of hundreds of species during the past 500 years.

Overexploitation

A species that is overexploited is one that has become endangered or extinct because it has been overused. For example, the unrestricted hunting of passenger pigeons caused that species' extinction. Unrestricted whaling during the twentieth century is another example, because humans hunted many whale species nearly to the point of extinction. This situation has been brought under control through the implementation of strict laws and an international moratorium on whaling. Because of the moratorium, several endangered whale species—such as the gray whale—have made comebacks.

Many animals are overexploited for specific animal parts. For example, humans poach (illegally hunt and capture) many species for their horns (rhino), tusks (elephant, walrus), bones (tiger), and skins (leopard). Many people illegally acquire these animal parts to sell to private collectors on the black market or to use in traditional medicines. We will look at poaching in more detail later in this chapter.

Disease

If a species does not have the natural genetic protection against particular pathogens (disease-causing agents), an introduced disease can have severe effects on that species since it has no resistance to the disease. For example, domesticated animals often transmit the diseases that affect wild populations.

Pollution

Pollution has had a serious adverse effect on many land-based and water-based animal species. Pollution can come in many forms. Household trash (paper, plastics, food, bottles, and cans) pollute the environment when improperly dumped. Many birds become entangled every year in the thin plastic rings that hold six-packs together. If animals eat the plastic, it can suffocate them or block their digestive tract and make them starve to death; or can strangle them if they get the plastic rings entwined around their necks or trap them. Plastic products do not biodegrade quickly, either. Plastic six-pack rings can last more than 400 years in the ocean. (Six-pack rings should be cut up before discarding so that they do not function as a noose.)

Sulfur dioxide—a gas produced by burning oil and coal—in the atmosphere, leads to acid rain that falls back to Earth as snow, rain, or fog. Pesticides used on farms and in gardens pollute the natural environment when they get into water and the surrounding soil. Chemical waste from industries can also make its way into groundwater and contaminate the ecosystem.

Chemicals, such as DDT (an insecticide used in the 1960s), have also polluted the environment and caused major problems to the health of some species. By the time DDT entered the animals at the top of the food chain—such as the bald eagle—the chemical was so concentrated in their food that it drastically affected their ability to produce offspring, thereby threatening them with extinction. This is why DDT was banned in the early 1970s and has been illegal in the United States since.

Habitat Fragmentation

When an animal's habitat becomes threatened by the above-mentioned conditions, this can destroy large areas of habitat. Habitat can become fragmented, or broken up, into many small concentrations instead of one large area. When habitat becomes fragmented, it can continue until the habitat—and the species—are eliminated. Also, if animal habitats get fragmented enough, this adversely affects the gene pool, and species can die out because of the insufficient variability of genes for reproduction.

CONSERVATION PLANNING AND ENVIRONMENTAL IMPACT ANALYSIS

The most important step humans can take is to stop the destruction of habitats and to try to repair as much of the damage already done as possible. This includes stopping the following: the introduction of exotic species; the cutting down of forests; littering; polluting the air, water, and land; introducing disease; and exploiting wildlife.

Active measures are needed if biodiversity is going to be conserved for future generations. Conservation planning is a critical step necessary to accomplish these goals. Specific areas can be designated for conservation and monitoring in the form of official reserves. The first step is to identify areas and designate a network of nature reserves. These areas set aside for nature must also be protected, managed, and if necessary, restored.

In order to effectively preserve areas, managers must have a plan set in place to achieve this goal. Sometimes the area that is set aside for protection is not large enough to support all the functions of a natural ecosystem. Good management practices are needed to fulfill those functions. For example, effective management may include the removal of exotic species, having controlled burns, improving stream quality, or reforesting areas with native species. These actions must be documented in a management plan so that progress can be monitored and improved where necessary.

These areas may also need to be protected, for example, from poaching by requiring the posting of guards in the area. An area may need to be fenced in. Hunting, logging, farming, and urbanization are all activities that can threaten the health of an ecosystem if nothing is done to control or prevent them. For this reason, many parks, reserves, and refuges have been designated in the United States. The roles of these areas will be discussed in greater detail in the next chapter.

It is necessary for managers to analyze environmental impacts when a specific use for the land is proposed. For example, when building an urban area, it is important to analyze the effects building will have on the land (erosion and destruction of vegetation), the water (chemicals, other pollutants, overuse, and diversion), and air (pollution).

When cutting down trees in a forest, managers need to know beforehand what effects it will have on the soil, such as loss of nutrients, erosion, and nonproductivity, as well as which animals in the food chain it will affect. In farming, managers must analyze how their water use will reduce the normal flow of water that sustains wildlife; what effect pesticides, herbicides, and other pollutants will have; and the impact of introducing certain crops in place of the natural vegetation.

All possible impacts need to be studied and analyzed before a change in land use occurs. If it is determined that the environmental impacts will harm an ecosystem, then alternative plans can be looked at in order to prevent short- or long-term damage to the area and its complex ecosystem.

THE TRUTH ABOUT POACHING

Poaching is illegal hunting or fishing. Numerous state and federal laws protect wildlife, including endangered species, but there is still a large business in trafficking the skins, meat, and other parts of illegally killed wild animals. Organized poaching threatens a number of species with extinction—especially those that have valuable body parts. Unfortunately, the rarer the species, the more valuable its carcass is in the black market.

Some animal parts are valued as ornaments, such as ivory from elephant or walrus tusks, or skin from lizards, crocodiles, tigers, and polar bears. Even though polar bears are protected by a number of laws

Poaching is a serious problem for several species. Walruses (a) and elephants (b) are sought after for their tusks. In order to obtain the tusks, the animal must be killed. Although it is illegal, it is difficult to control in some countries. *(Courtesy of the U.S. Fish and Wildlife Service)*

and international treaties, they are still taken illegally in some sections of their Arctic range, such as in remote areas of the Russian Arctic. Tusk ivory can be carved into many shapes and objects, such as statues, jewelry, flatware handles, furniture inlays, and piano keys. Warthog tusks and teeth from sperm whales, orcas, and hippos can be scrimshawed, or carved into what some perceive as art.

Other parts are valued for use in traditional medicine—particularly in Asia—such as tiger bones, animal genitals, and the horn of the rhinoceros. According to the U.S. Fish and Wildlife Service, animal smuggling has become a multinational industry valued at roughly $30 billion a year.

In addition, animals perceived to be dangerous to humans (or their livestock), such as bears, tigers, wolves, lions, and cougars, are also threatened by illegal hunting. Another type of poaching involves the capture of live animals for the pet trade or for use as performing animals. Sometimes the adult animals are deliberately killed in order to capture their young. Often, only a small number of the animals captured will survive to be sold. Animals such as parrots, reptiles, primates, and invertebrates are common targets for the pet trade. Animals that are sometimes taken to serve as performing animals include bears and monkeys.

Another aspect of poaching involves the poachers who sell bush meat to the huge market of poor rural Africans who do not have access to domestic meat. In central Africa alone, it is estimated that more than one million metric tons of wildlife are killed for meat each year—the equivalent of four million cattle. In addition to law enforcement, another possible solution lies in education. Many of the isolated tribes and villages in Africa are not aware that their wildlife is more valuable to them alive than dead. Wildlife education programs have been shown to be successful in curbing poaching and leading to legislation that restricts hunting.

The United States was one of the 95 nations that signed a treaty and joined a group aimed at stopping the illegal trade in rare animals and plants. Starting in 1973, the Convention on International

Illegal Animal Products

Animal	Region of the world	Product
Elephant	Asia, Africa	Tusks for ivory, hide for boots, feet for waste baskets
Walrus	Arctic waters	Tusks for ivory
Sea turtle	Warm-water oceans	Shell for jewelry, skin for leather
Polar bear	Arctic	Rugs
Grizzly	North America	Rugs, jaws, claws, teeth
Rhinoceros	Asia, Africa	Medicine (Rhino horn has been used as an ingredient in traditional Asian medicine for the past 2,000 years.) and horn for daggers
Leopard	Africa	Fur coats, teeth
Jaguar	South America	Fur coats
Tiger	Asia	Skins

Trade in Endangered Species of Wild Flora and Fauna (called CITES) has met yearly. Not all countries enforce their laws to ban poaching. Unfortunately, there are always collectors who are willing to buy these poached items, which increases the smuggling of illegal goods. Without collectors willing to buy, the smuggling could be controlled.

THE ENVIRONMENTAL EFFECTS OF OIL SPILLS ON WILDLIFE

Oil spills into rivers, bays, and the ocean are caused by accidents involving tankers, barges, pipelines, refineries, and storage facilities. Spills happen usually when the oil is being transported. Spills can be caused by people making mistakes, equipment failure, natural disasters such as hurricanes, or deliberate acts by terrorists or countries at war.

Oil floats on salt water (the ocean) and usually floats on fresh water (rivers and lakes). Oil usually spreads out rapidly across the water surface to form a thin layer called an oil slick. As the oil continues to spread further, the layer becomes thinner until it is a very thin layer called a sheen, which often looks like a rainbow (sheens are sometimes visible on roads or in parking lots after a rain).

Depending on the circumstances, oil spills can be very harmful to marine birds and mammals, such as sea otters. They can also harm fish and shellfish. Oil destroys the insulating ability of fur-bearing mammals, such as sea otters, and the water-repelling abilities of a bird's feathers, thereby exposing these creatures to the harsh elements. Many birds and animals also ingest (swallow) oil when they try to clean themselves, which can poison them. Depending on the circumstances—where and when a spill happens—from just a few up to hundreds or thousands of birds and mammals can be killed or injured. Oftentimes, rescue workers set up stations where they can clean and rehabilitate wildlife. The U.S. Fish and Wildlife Service is often called in to help.

How spilled oil affects near-surface creatures depends on when and where the oil spills. Because the condition at the surface of the ocean is always changing—flocks of seabirds come and go; plankton are more

Oil spills from tankers are extremely harmful to wildlife. (a) Cleanup of an Amoco oil spill along the coast; (b) Oil spills in wetlands and other fragile ecosystems can destroy habitat; (c) Sea otters are one species that can be harmed from an oil spill. Oil coats their fur and causes them to lose their ability to keep warm. Also, if they groom their fur and ingest the oil, it can kill them; (d) Oil spills can be extremely hazardous to birds. These ducks died because their feathers became too saturated with oil. *(a and c, courtesy of the National Oceanic and Atmospheric Administration (NOAA); b, courtesy of the U.S. Fish and Wildlife Service, Luther Goldman; d, courtesy of the U.S. Fish and Wildlife Service)*

numerous at certain times than others—the surface might have sparse populations of living organisms, or it could have dense populations.

How oil affects near-surface creatures also depends on how vulnerable those animals are to the effects of oil. Birds that float on the water surface and dive to feed can be oiled if they happen to be in the same place as an oil slick. Seabirds keep themselves warm by means of their feathers, so when they get oiled, the birds get hypothermia (their body temperature gets too low) and often die. Since birds preen themselves to clean their feathers, they can also ingest the oil, which can either make them sick or kill them.

Marine mammals—such as seals, whales, or porpoises—must come to the surface in order to breathe. If they become oiled, this may irritate their eyes or skin, or they may breathe in harmful oil fumes. Seals and sea lions are especially at risk of oiling when their pupping areas have been oiled.

Some mammals can be much more seriously harmed, however. While most seals, whales, and porpoises keep themselves warm by having thick layers of blubber, otters and fur seals keep themselves warm by having thick fur coats. Because of this, otters and fur seals are much more vulnerable to oil than other marine mammals. When the fur of an otter or fur seal gets oiled and matted, it can no longer warm the animal, and the animal will soon die of hypothermia. This is what makes fur-bearing mammals and seals, along with sea birds, so vulnerable to oil impacts.

Spilled oil can also affect creatures below the surface of the ocean. A small percentage of the spilled oil will disperse naturally down into the water column. This dispersing oil can affect creatures that live there, such as fish and plankton. Some animals may be able to avoid the oil by swimming away from it, such as fish. Others, such as plankton (tiny plants and animals that drift with the currents), may be hurt or killed by oil in the water column.

Because of the susceptibility of animals to oil spills, it is important that oil shipping be managed carefully. If a spill does occur, there needs to be rescue and clean up plans in place to manage the restoration of the natural environment.

LAWS THAT PROTECT ENDANGERED SPECIES

Half of the recorded extinction of mammals over the past 2,000 years have occurred in the most recent 50-year period. The Endangered Species Act is a law that was passed by Congress and signed by President Nixon in 1973. It is regarded as one of the most comprehensive wildlife conservation laws in the world. In 1973, 109 species were listed. Today, over 1,000 species are listed.

Congress had enacted two similar laws—one in 1966 and another in 1969—but neither did more than create lists of vanishing wildlife species. This was no better than publishing a list of crime victims but doing nothing to catch the criminals. The Endangered Species Act in 1973, however, changed all that by setting very specific guidelines. It forbids people from trapping, harming, harassing, poisoning, wounding, capturing, hunting, collecting, importing, exporting, or in any other way harming any species of animal or plant whose continued existence is threatened. The U.S. Fish and Wildlife Service manages the listing of land and freshwater species. The Natural Marine Fisheries Service (NMFS) is in charge of ocean species.

This act protects all species classified as threatened or endangered, whether they have commercial value (where people want to buy, sell, and collect them) or not. It also forbids federal participation in projects that jeopardize listed species and calls for the protection of all habitat critical to listed species.

Under this law, the term "endangered" designates a species in danger of extinction throughout all or a significant part of its range. "Threatened" refers to species likely to become endangered in the foreseeable future. The Fish and Wildlife Service also maintains a list of "candidate" species. These are species that have not yet been proposed for listing but which the Service has enough information about to warrant proposing them for listing as endangered or threatened. The protection also extends to the preservation of the species' habitats. Assistance is provided to states and foreign governments to assure this protection.

The law's ultimate goal is to "recover" species so they no longer need protection under the Endangered Species Act. The law provides for recovery plans to be developed describing the steps needed to restore a species to health. Public and private agencies, institutions, and scientists assist in the development and implementation of recovery plans.

The Endangered Species Act is the law that puts into effect U.S. participation in the Convention of International Trade in Endangered Species of Wild Fauna and Flora (CITES)—a 130-nation agreement designed to prevent species from becoming endangered or extinct because of international trade.

There are some exceptions to the protection provided by the Endangered Species Act. Natives of Alaska can hunt endangered animals for use as food or shelter. An endangered animal can also be killed if it threatens the life of a human or if it is too sick to survive.

Conservationists agree that it is in the best interests of mankind to minimize the loss of genetic variation. All life on Earth is an important resource. Many species—even those unknown at this point—could provide answers to questions and solutions to problems in the future. If humans destroy species now, they may never understand the potential of these species as natural resources.

In addition to the Endangered Species Act, several other species-specific protection laws have been put into place. These laws are described below.

The Bald and Golden Eagle Protection Act

This act makes it illegal to import, export, or take bald or golden eagles. It is also illegal to sell, purchase, or barter their parts or products made from them, including their nests or eggs. Possession of a feather or other body part of a bald eagle is a felony with a fine of up to $10,000 and/or imprisonment.

The bald eagle was one of the species adversely affected during the 1960s with the use of the insecticide DDT. Because they ingested high levels of DDT through the food chain, it seriously impacted their ability to produce offspring. Since DDT was banned and laws have been put in place to protect the bald eagle, it has made a remarkable comeback.

The Migratory Bird Treaty Act

This act was born in an era when people adorned their hats with egret feathers and signed their letters with pelican-quill pens. This law was first introduced in 1918 and was an agreement between the United States and Great Britain for the protection of birds migrating between the United States and Canada. Similar agreements followed after that on the part of the United States, Mexico, Japan, and Russia. This act made it illegal for people to pursue, kill, hunt, capture, possess, buy, sell, purchase, or barter any migratory bird, including the feathers or other parts, nests, eggs, or migratory bird products. In total, 836 bird species are protected by the act. A migratory bird is any species or family of birds that live, reproduce, or migrate within or across international borders at some point during their annual life cycle.

The Marine Mammal Protection Act

In 1972, this act was passed by Congress to protect the many mammals that live in the world's oceans. This legislation is the basis for policies preventing the harassment, capture, injury, or killing of all species of whales, dolphins, seals, and sea lions, as well as walruses, manatees, dugongs, sea otters, and polar bears.

This law helps manage the interaction of marine mammals with fisheries so that mortalities and injuries are reduced—such as preventing marine mammals from getting entangled in fishermen's gear. It also regulates scientific research in the wild; establishes basic requirements for public display of captive marine mammals, such as orcas, dolphins, walruses, and seals; and addresses issues with the tuna industry and their trapping methods to ensure the safety of dolphins. This act is enforced by the National Marine Fisheries Service (NMFS), which is within the Department of Commerce, National Oceanic and Atmospheric Administration (NOAA).

The National Wildlife Refuge System Administration Act

This act was created in 1966 and serves as the "organic act" for the National Wildlife Refuge System. This act provides guidelines and directives for the administration and management of all areas in the system, such as wildlife refuges, areas for the protection and conservation of fish and wildlife that are threatened with extinction, wildlife ranges, game ranges, wildlife management areas, and waterfowl production areas.

According to the U.S. Fish and Wildlife Service, as of January 1999, 56 refuges have been acquired nationally, principally under the authority of the Endangered Species Act, for the benefit of threatened and endangered species. Examples of these refuges include Hakalau Forest (endangered Hawaiian birds); Crystal River, Florida (manatees); Buenos Aires, Arizona (masked bobwhite quail); and the Oklahoma Bat Caves (endangered bats). Over 600 national wildlife refuges, wetland management districts, and wildlife coordination areas contribute to the well-being of endangered and threatened species.

The Lacey Act

This act provides authority to the U.S. Secretary of the Interior to designate injurious wildlife and ensure the humane treatment of wildlife shipped to the United States. It stops the importing, exporting, transportation, sale, or purchase of fish and wildlife taken or possessed in violation of state, federal, tribal, and foreign laws. It helps enforce federal wildlife laws and improve federal assistance to the states and foreign governments to help enforce their wildlife laws. It also helps control the smuggling and trade in the poaching of fish and wildlife.

The Airborne Hunting Act

This act—also called the Shooting from Aircraft Act—prohibits the taking or harassing of wildlife from aircraft, except when protecting wildlife, livestock, and human health or safety, as authorized by a federal or state issued license or permit.

The Antarctic Conservation Act

This act provides for the conservation and protection of the animals and plants of Antarctica and the ecosystems in which these species live. It makes it illegal for any U.S. citizen to take any native bird or mammal in Antarctica or to collect any native plants from any specially protected area within Antarctica. This act also makes it illegal for any U.S. citizen or any foreign person in the United States to possess, sell, offer for sale, deliver, receive, carry, transport, import, export, or attempt to import or export from the United States any native mammal or bird taken in Antarctica or any plant collected in any specially protected area.

The African Elephant Conservation Act

The purpose of this act is to provide additional protection for the African elephant. The act establishes an assistance program to the elephant producing countries of Africa and provides for the establishment of an African Elephant Conservation Fund. The act also places a moratorium on the importation of raw, or worked, ivory from African elephant producing countries.

The Wild Bird Conservation Act of 1992

This act promotes the conservation of exotic birds by encouraging wild bird conservation and management programs in the countries of origin. It ensures that all trade involving these birds in the United States is biologically sustainable and to the benefit of the species. It also limits or prohibits imports of exotic birds when necessary to ensure that exotic wild populations are not harmed by removal for the trade.

Having management laws like these in place is the first step toward protecting wildlife species. The next steps, as we will see in Chapter 8, include the maintenance of refuges and preserves, recovery plans, captive breeding, the contributions of zoos, and the critical role of designated wilderness areas in order to ensure the future of each species.

CONSERVATION OF ANIMAL RESOURCES

This chapter addresses the conservation of animal resources. It discusses why it is important to save endangered species, the steps that lead to extinction, and the true costs related to this problem. It then covers the TESS List—the list that officially identifies threatened and endangered species—and how species become listed as endangered. Next it identifies the myths and realities of the Endangered Species Act and reminds us that extinction means forever.

This chapter also highlights several endangered species and their plights. It then focuses on conservation, planning, and restoration of species and their habitats through the utilization of refuges, recovery plans, reintroduction to the wild, zoos, captive breeding, and wetlands management and preservation. The critical role of designated, undisturbed wilderness areas and why it is important to keep the "wild" in wilderness are also explored.

ANIMALS ARE A PRECIOUS RESOURCE

Species are an integral part of whole, interacting ecosystems. Ecosystems provide habitat for species, climate control, and nutrient recycling. These whole systems must be conserved, protected, and preserved. When a species is listed as endangered, it is in immediate danger of extinction. When any extinction occurs, it affects the Earth's biodiversity negatively and irreversibly. When a species is lost, knowledge of its historic relationship to local and global environmental factors is also lost.

Some people argue that extinction is a natural process—species have been going extinct throughout the history of the Earth—so there may not be a critical need to save endangered species. Today, however, the process of extinction is not natural. Most plant and animal species become extinct due to habitat destruction, overharvesting, introduction of nonnative species, and other processes that have a direct or indirect link to human activity. It is the human factor that is putting so many animals at risk by threatening their survival. Today, extinction rates are 100 to 1,000 times higher than pre-human levels.

The reality is that animal species are a critically valuable resource for many reasons. At least one-third of agricultural crops depend on insect and other animal pollinators for their reproduction—which means our food supply, and survival, depend on the health of these pollinators.

Animals provide ecological benefits. Many people tend to take nature for granted and assume that the ecosystem services that we depend on will continue regardless of which human activities are taking place. But when species become endangered, it means that the health of the ecosystem is deteriorating. There are also aesthetic and spiritual benefits related to animals. Many people feel a close tie with nature and find it soothing and rejuvenating.

Wild species have proved to be valuable sources of new medicines as well as medical models that help scientists understand how the human body works. At least one-fourth of all prescriptions written each year in the United States contain chemicals discovered in plants and animals. If these species had been destroyed before their chemistries were known, their secrets would have died with them. For example, the endangered Arizona pupfish, which has an amazing ability to adapt to high salt concentrations, is proving useful for research into human kidney disease.

Maintaining biological diversity benefits humanity. Throughout time, animals and plants have provided humans with food, clothing, energy, medicines, and other important items. Conserving biological diversity is essential for maintaining intact ecosystems. There may exist today an animal species that could present a solution to medical science for cancer or any number of life-threatening illnesses. Scientists have determined that the disappearance of just one plant species can take with it up to 30 other species, including insects, higher animals, and other plants.

There are also unrecognized benefits of maintaining biological diversity, such as the services we receive when an ecosystem functions normally. These include chemical cycling (oxygen production), maintenance and generation of soil, and groundwater recharge. An example of problems caused by ecosystem degradation and species endangerment is the loss of much of the Everglades wetlands. Problems in water quality and quantity for natural and human systems and declines in fish and wildlife populations have all been linked to the drainage of the Everglades. Unfortunately, the costs of fixing these problems are tremendous—it ranges in the hundreds of millions of dollars.

Species are also important indicators of environmental quality. Endangered species can act as a warning sign when something is wrong in our ecosystems. For example, the dangers of DDT became evident with the rapid decline in numbers of bald eagles and peregrine falcons. If DDT had not been barred, it could have had detrimental effects on humans. Even nonendangered species can be used as indicators of environmental quality. For example, largemouth bass and other sport fish have warned humans of mercury contamination in freshwater ecosystems. The spread of cattails into freshwater marshes that used to be dominated by other species of grass warn people of nutrient problems.

The conservation of animal species is a challenge that must be addressed by both the public (government) sector and the private sector. It takes federal, state, regional, and local agencies working together with other citizens to give certain species of wildlife a better chance of survival.

Humans need to find ways to support and preserve endangered species and realize that in doing so, everyone benefits—both humans and wildlife species. Benefits of species can be classified as ecological, economic, and social.

As identified by the National Wildlife Federation, specific human activities that threaten and endanger wildlife include the following:

- Habitat loss and degradation
- Invasive species
- Global warming
- Pollution
- Pesticides
- Human population growth
- Agriculture
- Logging and fire suppression
- Mining and drilling
- Poaching
- Overfishing
- Urbanization
- Damming and channelizing rivers

Because of the increasing human population, significant portions of the land and water on Earth have been degraded. These transformations can cause many species to die out.

Invasive species are harmful, nonnative animals, microorganisms, and plants that humans introduced into an environment in which they did not evolve. Usually, they have no natural enemies to limit their reproduction and therefore spread rapidly. These exotic invaders comprise the second largest threat to global diversity, after habitat loss. The damage that invasive species cause to agriculture, forestry, fisheries, property, and human health are estimated at $137 billion each year.

Global warming threatens endangered species because, as global warming alters temperatures, humidity, soil and vegetation, it can ruin a habitat for an endangered species that has a limited natural range. In addition, endangered species often depend on one or a few species for food, some of which are also vulnerable to global warming.

Pollution from agricultural, industrial, and urban development threatens both terrestrial and aquatic species. Chemicals—such as those used in agriculture—are absorbed by surrounding plants, animals, and soils. These chemicals can alter soil and water composition and prove harmful—sometimes fatal—to many animal species.

Pesticide use also threatens wildlife. More than one billion pounds (450,000 kg) of pesticides are used each year on farms, ranches, lawns, and golf courses across the United States. Some pesticides affect the neurological and behavioral development in mammals, fish, amphibians, reptiles, and birds. Herbicides can be hazardous to mammals' reproduction, causing small mammals to have reduced litter sizes and deformed young.

Human population growth and consumption cause many problems. These problems include habitat fragmentation, deforestation, species extinction, water scarcity, loss of biodiversity, climate change, and pollution.

Agriculture requires converting native prairie (grasslands), grassland, forest, and wetlands to croplands. Agricultural practices can reduce the supply of water to wildlife species. Establishing a monoculture (growing only one crop) also removes important food sources that wildlife may depend on.

Logging forests not only eliminates forest habitat, it can increase stream bank erosion, making waterways uninhabitable for aquatic species. Fire suppression (keeping natural fires from burning) can also prove detrimental to animals. Small, natural fires help clear out the forest, which can prevent the spread of large, intense fires that can destroy trees.

Mining, oil and gas extraction, and geothermal exploration not only destroy beautiful habitats, but also pollute the area with acidic mine runoff, silt, noise, and debris. Access roadways must also be constructed, furthering habitat destruction.

As we saw in the previous chapter, poaching threatens the existence of animals. Poaching has driven many species to extinction.

Overfishing has contributed to the dramatic decline of wild salmon and many other fish. The global fishing industry captures about 60 billion pounds (27 billion kg) of fish each year that were not meant to be caught. According to the National Wildlife Federation, an estimated 150,000 sea turtles drown in shrimp trawl nets each year.

Urbanization is another major cause of species endangerment. When industrial buildings, homes, and roads are built, it takes away from species habitat because it changes how the land is used. This also ends up fragmenting habitats and forces species into smaller and smaller areas. When species become isolated, they can die from overpopulation in the smaller areas. They are also hurt because the gene pool becomes too restricted.

Many aquatic species are jeopardized when humans channel rivers and build dams. Dams keep many species from being able to migrate. They also change the water levels, gas concentrations, sedimentation, and temperature. Rivers are channelized to reduce flooding, but this also keeps necessary nutrients from the soils during the natural flood cycle and can destroy streamside areas for the species that live there.

All of these impacts from human activities threaten the health, future, and existence of animals. There are several steps to extinction—it doesn't just happen overnight. Wildlife biologists and the U.S. Fish and Wildlife Service have identified the key phases most species go through before they become extinct:

- Rare species: A plant or animal species whose population is small and isolated. Not many of its members can be seen in the wild, but its population is stable.

- Threatened or vulnerable species: A plant or animal species that may be abundant in some areas, but that still faces serious threats. It is likely to become endangered in the near future.
- Endangered: A plant or animal species whose numbers have been reduced to such an extent that it is in immediate danger of becoming extinct. Such a species needs help from humans to survive.
- Extinct: A plant or animal species that no longer exists. No individual members can be found alive anywhere.

Determining current and past extinction rates involves careful scientific study and calculations, by using the fossil record and measurements of habitat destruction. Fossil records can reveal the average lifetimes of species, or how long different classes of plants and animals generally exist on the Earth before going extinct. From this information, scientists can determine a basic rate of extinction—or the natural rate of extinction without human intervention. Once scientists calculate the base rate of extinction, it allows them to see how much faster species are becoming extinct in modern times due to the interference of humans.

The key factor is to be able to identify these phases of extinction and catch and reverse the damage at the beginning stages. By waiting longer to address a problem, the closer a species gets to extinction the more difficult it is to repair and reverse the damage.

According to the U.S. Fish and Wildlife Service, it is important to save species because protecting endangered species also protects humans as well as a healthy environment. Endangered species are nature's "911" because they are an early warning sign for pollution and environmental degradation that can affect human health. When people see certain animal species becoming sick, that is a signal that humans may also become sick if the environmental condition is not fixed.

Protecting endangered species also helps sustain the local economy and provides a good quality of life. Healthy environments sustain a variety of jobs—for example, commercial fishing, tourism, outdoor equipment sales, and clothing sales. Loss of forests and degradation of rivers and streams causes job losses. Americans spend more than $85 billion each year on fish and wildlife related recreation.

Protecting endangered species is also a fundamental American value. Protecting them saves a part of America's natural legacy, which can be left for future generations to enjoy. Americans do not turn away from something that is worth doing—even if it might be difficult. They are proud of saving the bald eagle and look forward to other successes. Many Americans regret the losses of important parts of our natural heritage—such as the extinction of the passenger pigeon. So why save endangered species? Because we can.

THE TESS LIST

Before a plant or animal species can receive protection under the Endangered Species Act, it must first be placed on the federal list of endangered and threatened wildlife and plants, maintained by the U.S. Fish and Wildlife Service. The listing program follows a strict legal process to determine whether to list a species, depending on the degree of threat it faces. An "endangered" species is one that is in danger of extinction throughout all or a significant portion of its range. A "threatened" species is one that is likely to become endangered in the foreseeable future. The U.S. Fish and Wildlife Service also maintains a list of plants and animals native to the United States that are candidates or proposed for possible addition to the federal list. All of the Fish and Wildlife Service's actions—from proposals to listings to removals (delisting) are announced through a publication called the *Federal Register* (a daily publication of the federal government).

The report, which lists all of the threatened and endangered species, is called the TESS List—for Threatened and Endangered Species Database System. The table on page 139 is a summary of listed threatened and endangered species, as well as how many U.S. species have recovery plans in place.

Candidate species are those plants and animals that the U.S. Fish and Wildlife Service has enough information on, regarding their

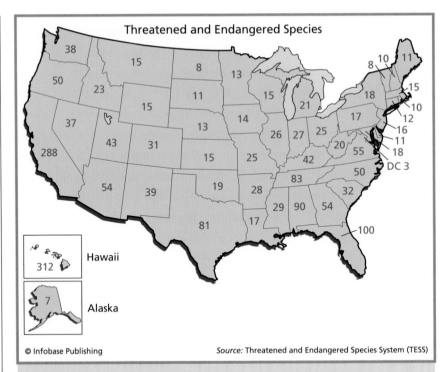

Threatened and Endangered Species

38 15 8 13 10 11 8 50 23 15 15 18 15 37 15 11 13 14 21 17 12 43 31 16 288 26 27 25 11 20 55 18 54 39 15 25 42 50 DC 3 19 28 83 32 29 90 54 81 17 100

312 Hawaii

7 Alaska

© Infobase Publishing   *Source:* Threatened and Endangered Species System (TESS)

Threatened and Endangered Species listed on the TESS list by state.

biological status and threats, in order to propose them as endangered or threatened under the Endangered Species Act, but which are not yet listed because other species are seen as higher priorities. A species is added to the list when it is determined to be endangered or threatened because of any of the following factors:

- The present or threatened destruction of the species' habitat or range
- Overuse of the species for commercial, recreational, scientific, or educational purposes
- Disease or predation
- Existing regulations that are not protecting the species
- Other natural or man-made factors that affect the species' survival

To list a species, several steps are followed in order to make it legal. The first step is to publish a "notice of review" that assesses the condition of a species. If the species meets the criteria, it becomes a candidate for listing. Through notices of review, the federal government collects information that will allow the species to be evaluated. The reviews are posted in the *Federal Register*.

Because of the large number of candidates and the time required to list a species, the Fish and Wildlife Service has developed a priority system designed to prioritize the plants and animals according to the greatest need for preservation.

Once a species is proposed in the *Federal Register*, any interested person can comment and provide additional information on the

Worldwide Threatened and Endangered Species

Group	Endangered in the U.S.	Endangered foreign	Threatened U.S.	Threatened foreign	Total species	U.S. species with recovery plans
Mammals	69	251	9	17	346	55
Birds	77	175	14	6	272	78
Reptiles	14	64	22	15	115	33
Amphibians	12	8	9	1	30	14
Fishes	71	11	43	0	125	95
Clams	62	2	8	0	72	69
Snails	21	1	11	0	33	23
Insects	35	4	9	0	48	31
Arachnids	12	0	0	0	12	5
Crustaceans	18	0	3	0	21	13
Total	391	516	128	39	1,074	416

(Source: U.S. Fish and Wildlife Service)

proposal—usually during a 60-day review period—and submit statements at any public hearings that may be held. In order to inform the public of these special hearings, news releases and mailings are issued.

Once the government receives public comments, they are analyzed and considered in the final rule-making process. Within one year of a listing proposal, one of three possible courses of action is taken:

- A final listing rule is published.
- The proposal is withdrawn because the biological information does not support the listing.
- The proposal is extended for up to six months due to substantial disagreement within the scientific community concerning the need to list a species. After the six months, a determination is made.

When a species is approved for listing, the final listing rule becomes effective 30 days after publication in the *Federal Register*. After a species is listed, its status is reviewed at least every five years to determine if federal protection is still necessary.

THE MYTHS AND REALITIES ABOUT THE ENDANGERED SPECIES ACT

The U.S. Fish and Wildlife Service has identified common myths about endangered species. For example, some people believe that extinction is a "natural" process and that we should not worry about it. The reality is that while extinction in general may be a normal process, the high extinction rates that exist today are not. In many cases, the environment is changing so fast that species do not have time to adapt. Scientists have determined that a natural extinction rate is one species lost every 100 years. However, since the pilgrims landed at Plymouth Rock over 365 years ago, more than 500 North American species have become extinct—that is more than one species becoming extinct per year.

Another myth is that the Endangered Species Act is causing loss of jobs and economic strain in many areas of the country. The truth is that when economists from the Massachusetts Institute of Technology analyzed the economic impact of endangered species, they found that states with many listed species have economies just as strong as those areas that do not have endangered species.

Another myth is that billions of tax dollars are being spent on endangered species. The fact is that the annual budget for the nation-wide endangered species program is only about $60 million, which is roughly the equivalent of 23 cents per person in the United States. As a comparison—according to the U.S. Bureau of the Census—Americans spend over $8.2 billion on pets, pet food, and pet supplies.

Another myth is that most of the endangered species are worth-less, insignificant, or lower forms of life that have no value to human-ity. The truth is that size and emotional appeal have no bearing on species' importance.

Some people mistakenly believe that thousands of private citizens have been prosecuted for harming or killing endangered species, even when the killing occurred accidentally. The truth is that most of the people prosecuted under the Endangered Species Act are illegal wildlife traffickers who illegally and knowingly collect rare wildlife and plants to sell for personal profit.

Another myth is that many unsolvable conflicts with endangered species occur every year, stopping many valuable projects and hin-dering progress. The reality is that of the 225,403 projects that were reviewed from 1979 to 1996, only 37 development projects were halted. That is one project stopped for every 6,902 projects reviewed. In most cases, projects that were halted did proceed once the project design was modified to avoid endangering a species.

EXTINCTION MEANS FOREVER

As simple as those words may seem, they are true: Extinction does mean forever. This section highlights a few of the species that are listed as threatened or endangered.

The Bald Eagle

Bald eagles are found in North America, and they commonly roost in forest trees near streams or open water. They eat fish, rabbits, squirrels, and waterfowl and can live 25 to 30 years. Their chief threats are pollution—such as pesticides—and human encroachment. Bald eagles care for, and are very devoted to, their young. They build the largest nests in the world. The nest, made out of sticks and foliage, can get as big as 9 feet (2.74 m) around and 12 feet (3.66 m) deep. The nests are added to each year and can weigh more than 2,000 pounds (907.20 kg). They may be built 70 feet (21.34 m) above the ground, either in a treetop or on a cliff near the water.

Female bald eagles usually lay two eggs, which both parents **incubate** in turns until they hatch. During the first three months, the parents feed their young and teach them to fly and catch fish and other prey. Then the adults force the young out of the nest to find their own territory, because eagles need a large prey base and territory in order to survive. In recent years, bald eagles have begun to make a comeback, but they are not yet out of danger.

The Blue Whale

The blue whale is found in Arctic and Antarctic regions during the summer months and subtropical latitudes during the winter months. They live in deep ocean water and are the largest creatures on Earth. An adult blue whale can weigh 135 tons (122,472 kg) and can be 100 feet (30.48 m) long. They can live up to 80 years and survive on a diet of plankton and krill. The largest threat they face from humans is poaching for their blubber. Even after more than 20 years of bans on whaling, the world population of blue whales is fewer than 1,000 animals.

The Bongo Antelope

The bongo antelope lives in eastern, central, and western Africa, generally in lowland forests. They live for about 17 years and eat mainly grass. The biggest threats they face are habitat loss and poaching. The bongo antelope is a beautiful hoofed mammal with a rust-colored coat with thin, vertical white stripes.

The Florida Panther

The Florida panther is not a panther, but a large cat that belongs to the same family as the domestic cat. It is a subspecies of the cougar. The Florida panther is found only in Florida. At one time, panthers had a habitat range from the lower Mississippi valley through the panhandle of Florida to the Everglades. In 1995, only 30 to 50 Florida panthers remained, all in protected areas south of Lake Okeechobee. Young panthers stay with their mother for the first two years. Captive-breeding efforts are in progress for this panther. Ten kittens were caught in 1991 to establish a captive-breeding population, but intensive attempts to breed the panther have not proved successful. Their numbers are so low that inbreeding is causing serious genetic problems.

Human encroachment and overdevelopment are the two biggest reasons Florida panthers have become endangered. Conservationists are trying to establish enough protected areas so that the surviving cats will have adequate habitat for hunting and breeding. In 1989, the U.S. Fish and Wildlife Service established the 30,000-acre Florida Panther National Wildlife Refuge.

Hyacinth Macaw

The hyacinth macaw lives in east-central South America, primarily in swamps, forests, and palm groves. They can live up to 80 years and eat mainly seeds, nuts, and fruits. The chief threats they face are the pet trade and tropical rain forest destruction.

The hyacinth macaw is the largest of all parrots and is cobalt blue in color. They make their nests in the hollows of trees—preferably palm trees—that provide protection from predators. It is illegal to capture them in the wild and sell them as pets. Only parrots hatched in captivity are legal as pets.

Manatee

Manatees are huge, slow-moving aquatic mammals often referred to as sea cows. The manatee lives in the Caribbean from the southeastern United States to northern South America. They prefer to inhabit estuaries, coastal lagoons, and freshwater rivers. They eat sea grass and other aquatic plants. They can live up to 50 years in the wild. The biggest threat they face is habitat destruction due to the increasing use of boats with outboard motors. They are also poached for their hides. Even though they are a protected species, they are still endangered.

Peregrine Falcon

The peregrine falcon inhabits all continents on the Earth—except Antarctica—and many oceanic islands. It prefers to nest in high places, such as ledges, rocky cliffs, tall buildings, and occasionally trees. A bird of prey, it eats other birds and rodents. They can live up to 15 years, but the biggest challenge they face is pollution from pesticides.

Fortunately, the peregrine falcon is making a comeback. In the 1970s, the North American population was extinct east of the Mississippi River.

Birds of Prey

Birds of prey—also called raptors—include eagles, hawks, owls, and falcons. Raptors are perfectly designed for hunting. They have the best long-range vision of any creature on Earth. They can see at least eight times better than humans. In dim light, owls can see many times better than humans can. One reason raptors see so well is because their eyes are large. Their wings are also designed to help them hunt. They have long wings that help them soar and circle high in the air to look for prey. Owls can glide toward prey in total silence.

All birds of prey have four toes on each foot. The toes have curved **claws**—called talons—that are razor sharp. Raptors use their feet to grasp and stab or crush their prey. Raptors have upper beaks that are hooked and pointed for tearing up prey once they have killed it.

They were severely impacted by the use of the pesticide DDT. Today, however, by eliminating DDT from the environment and carrying on intensive captive breeding, the peregrine has begun to recover.

Koala Bear

The koala is a small, bearlike, tree-dwelling herbivorous marsupial found in Australia. The koala gets its name from an ancient Aboriginal word meaning "no drink," because it receives over 90% of its hydration from the eucalyptus leaves it eats. Koalas survive on a diet of eucalyptus leaves.

Since European settlement, roughly 80% of Australia's eucalyptus forests have been destroyed. The remaining 20% is not protected, and most occurs on privately owned land. The chief causes of habitat loss for the koala are the clearing of land for urbanization, agriculture, mining, and the construction of roads. Over 4,000 koalas are killed each year by dogs and cars. Koala populations have also become fragmented and are at risk of extinction from bushfires. A single fire can destroy an entire habitat, and bushfires are unfortunately very common in the summer months.

SUCCESS—ONE SPECIES AT A TIME

All of the plants and animals on the endangered species list require a dedicated effort to save. Each species is worth saving—not only for the sake of the species itself, but also to protect other components of the ecosystem. If the food chain is disrupted, this can eventually destroy an entire ecosystem. According to the U.S. Fish and Wildlife Service, the removal of just one species can have adverse effects on 30 other species that depend on the target species functioning in its niche.

Fortunately, through the dedicated conservation efforts of many scientists and the growing awareness of the public as they become more educated, there are a number of success stories where a species has been saved from extinction. Long-term conservation plans that are closely followed will help increase numbers of endangered species. The goal for any conservation program is to restore habitat and allow the animal to reproduce to the level that their existence is no longer in jeopardy. Each species that is saved is an important step forward, as illustrated by the following examples provided by the National Wildlife Federation.

Bald Eagle

There were once around 100,000 bald eagles inhabiting the lower 48 states before Columbus sailed to the Americas. By 1963, habitat loss, hunting, and pesticide contamination had reduced the number of surviving eagles to 417 nesting pairs. The U.S. Fish and Wildlife Service began a captive-breeding program and habitat protection. In 1972, the ban on the insecticide DDT also helped. Today, there are almost 6,500 pairs in the continental United States. As their numbers increase, they may eventually be delisted.

Gray Wolf

When settlers moved West in the United States, they killed so many gray wolves that by the 1930s they were nearly extinct in the lower 48 states. Settlers killed the wolves for eating their cattle and sheep. Ironically, the reason the wolf had to resort to preying on sheep and cattle is because the settlers had killed the wolf's major sources of food—the buffalo and elk.

The loss of wolves also had a negative effect on other animals—such as foxes and ravens—which ate the meat that wolves left behind after a kill. In order to save the wolves, the United States government released some into Yellowstone National Park. If a wolf gets out and kills any livestock, environmental groups pay ranchers for their losses. Because of these conservation efforts, the gray wolf is beginning to make a comeback.

Elephants

Elephant populations have decreased dramatically over the years because of poaching. Those who want their ivory tusks have killed much of the elephant population. The United States puts forth considerable efforts to make buying or selling elephant parts illegal.

The Rediscovery of the Ivory-Billed Woodpecker

The ivory-billed woodpecker once ranged from Texas to North Carolina, from southern Illinois through Florida, and south to Cuba. Its habitat was the swampy bottomland hardwood forests. These forests provided the woodpecker with its primary source of food: beetle larvae found under the bark of the old trees.

Two hundred years ago, the ivory-billed woodpecker had a habitat of 24 million acres, but now it has dwindled down to 4.4 million scattered acres. Most of the forests were cut down for timber and to convert the land use to agriculture. After the Civil War, timber companies from the North and Midwest—where forests were already cut—bought hundred-thousand-acre plots for as little as 12 cents an acre. Workers earning 50 cents a day manned the long crosscut saws that took down centuries-old trees in an hour.

Further destruction to the forests was caused when levees and dams were built along rivers. Without the water supply, the forests died off. Some animals went extinct, and many believed the ivory-billed woodpecker was one of them.

Then, a kayaker found trees that the bark had been scraped off of in the same pattern as was typical of an ivory-billed woodpecker. Encouraged, scientists set up remote cameras and sound recorders that would pick up the movements and sounds of the ivory-billed woodpecker approaching the tree. The cameras used an integrated infrared, heat-and-motion sensor with sensitivity settings that, when activated, caused the digital camera to take a picture. In February of 2004, the ivory-billed woodpecker was rediscovered.

The bird—believed to have been extinct for at least 60 years—has created a surge of optimism for scientists and conservationists. The U.S. Fish and Wildlife Service is combining efforts with conservation organizations that are now working together in a project called the Corridor of Hope Cooperative Conservation Plan to provide habitat and save the ivory-billed woodpecker from extinction. The Corridor of Hope is part of the Big Woods of Arkansas, an area 120 miles (193 km) long and up to 20 miles (32 km) wide in eastern Arkansas.

Federal funds will be used for research and monitoring, recovery planning, and public education. They will also be used to conserve habitat through conservation easements, safe-harbor agreements, and conservation reserves.

Rediscoveries of thought-to-be extinct species are rare. When they do happen, they provide encouragement for conservationists to pursue habitat protection.

(Source: U.S. Department of the Interior, People, Land, and Water, Vol. 11, No. 5, July 2005.)

Key Deer

A type of white-tailed deer, the key deer of Florida once had a habitat that covered the entire chain of islands off the south end of Florida, an area called the Florida Keys. Hunters overhunted the deer so that by 1950 there were only 25 left. This species was so devastated that it was one of the first species listed for protection in 1973. Because their habitat has been intensively protected and restored, today about 500 key deer exist.

Desert Tortoise

The desert tortoise has received a lot of attention recently. The biggest threat to the desert tortoise is disruption of its habitat by grazing, off-road vehicle traffic, mining, and vandalism. The U.S. Fish and Wildlife Service, the Bureau of Land Management, and the National Park Service all provide protection on public lands for desert tortoises.

Gray Bat

These bats were once very common in the southern and midwestern states. There were approximately 2.25 million living in the many limestone caverns in this region. Because of human activity and interference, there were then only about 128,000 by the time the species was finally listed as endangered in 1976. Because of this protection during the past 25 years, the bat population has increased dramatically. Today there are about 1.5 million bats in the habitat—another success story.

Piping Plover

The piping plover's habitat is along the Atlantic and Great Lakes shores and the banks of the midwestern rivers and lakes. Because of human activities, their population dropped to only 3,000 pairs total. The Endangered Species Act has helped to stabilize their habitat in order to enable them to start increasing in numbers.

In the 32 years since the Endangered Species Act was passed, many species have been saved from extinction, including:

American alligator

Bald eagle

Black-footed ferret

California condor

Chinook salmon

Grizzly bear (North American)

Key deer

Lynx

Masked bobwhite quail

Peregrine falcon

Desert tortoise

Florida manatee

Florida panther

Gray bat

Green sea turtle

Piping plover

Red-cockaded woodpecker

Short-nose sturgeon

Utah prairie dog

Whooping crane

Although saving endangered species takes a lot of coordination and dedication, it is a noteworthy accomplishment when species can be saved and even prosper. When even one species is lost, it can have a far-reaching negative impact. Every success marks a giant step in the right direction.

CONSERVATION, PLANNING, AND RESTORATION

Providing for healthy wildlife habitat requires careful planning and dedication. Conservationists have developed several ways to manage the land and provide for fragile, rare, threatened, and endangered species. This section addresses a few of them.

The key to successful planning, restoration, and conservation lies in the priority these are given in a society's value system. As illustrated in the figure on page 150, very little money is spent in the United States on wildlife conservation compared to entertainment and other commodities.

Refuges

All over North America, wildlife that was once shot or trapped year-round is now protected for at least part of each year by state and/or federal laws. Historically, it was overhunting that led to the establishment of the first federal wildlife refuges in the United States. The refuge system began because all wildlife—including game birds, such

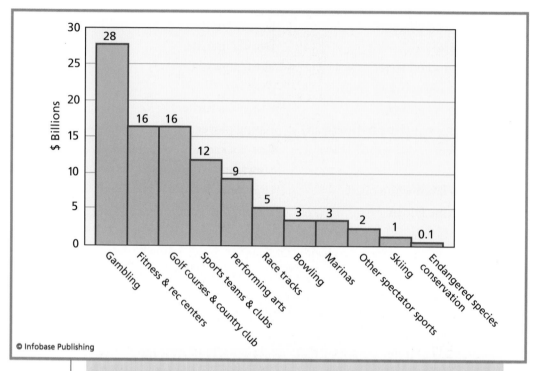

© Infobase Publishing

Annual American expenditures. Note the high expenditures (in billions of dollars) for recreational activities compared to what is allocated toward endangered species conservation efforts by the U.S. Fish and Wildlife Service. In comparison to recreational activities, very little is actually spent toward wildlife (and plant) conservation efforts. *(Sources of data: U.S. Bureau of the Census and U.S. Fish and Wildlife Service)*

as ducks, geese and other species of migratory waterfowl—were being slaughtered. President Theodore Roosevelt realized that waterfowl needed safe places along their migration routes. By 1904, 51 refuges had been set aside in the United States and its territories. Many were mainly waterfowl habitats, but some were for the benefit of nongame birds, like pelicans and spoonbills.

Today, there are more than 440 federal wildlife refuges totaling 92 million acres. Most of the acreage is in Alaska, but refuges are located all over the United States and its territories.

The Florida panther is a critically endangered species. It is believed that there are fewer than 50 of these animals remaining. *(Courtesy of the U.S. Fish and Wildlife Service, by George Gentry)*

Also, many national parks, forests, and monuments, plus thousands of state and county parks and reserves, and many privately owned preserves provide habitat for wildlife in the United States. Millions of acres have been set aside for the protection of wild animals and plants. Many environmental groups, ecologists, and private citizens would like to see more land set aside for these efforts. It often takes many years of public education and political lobbying in order to establish new reserves to protect wildlife. It is an effort well rewarded to promote species diversity.

Recovery Plans

Recovery plans are put in place to save endangered species. The U.S. Fish and Wildlife Service and the National Oceanic and Atmospheric

A photo gallery of some endangered animal species. (a) Green sea turtle; (b) Nene; (c) Wood stork; (d) Gray wolf; (e) California condor; (f) Bengal tiger. *(Courtesy of the U.S. Fish and Wildlife Service; a,c by Ryan Hagerty; b, Lee Karney; d, William C. Campbell; e, Scott Frier; f, Ron Singer)*

Administration (which includes the National Marine Fisheries Service) are the two agencies charged with the administration and implementation of the Endangered Species Act. The ultimate goal of the Endangered Species Act is the recovery of listed species and their associated ecosystems to levels where protection under the Act is no longer necessary.

According to the U.S. Fish and Wildlife Service, a variety of methods and procedures are used to recover listed species, such as protective measures to prevent extinction or further decline; consultation to avoid adverse impacts of federal activities; habitat acquisition and restoration; captive breeding; and other on-the-ground activities for managing and monitoring endangered and threatened species. It is also important for other organizations to work along with the federal government to enable these recovery plans to be effective. For example, efforts provided by state and local government agencies, tribal governments, the business community, landowners, and other concerned citizens are critical to the recovery of listed species.

When recovery plans are put in place, they must ensure coordinated, effective recovery actions as well as actions to reverse the decline of the species. Recovery plans—documents prepared for listed species that detail the specific tasks needed for recovery—provide a realistic way for private, federal, and state organizations to work together. A plan may cover one or several species.

Recovery programs do work, but recovery is a challenge that takes time in order to successfully halt and reverse the decline of the endangered species. Recovery takes a long time because it must reverse declines that may have been going on for two hundred years or more. The recovery period also depends on the status of the species' population, the **gestation** rate of a species, or other biological factors.

Of all the species listed between 1968 and 2000, only seven (less than 1%) have been recognized as extinct. Almost 99% of listed species have not become extinct due to the success of the Endangered Species Act and effective recovery plans.

Reintroduction to the Wild

Sometimes, wildlife biologists help once-scarce species by releasing individuals in places where populations have been previously wiped out. This was done with wild turkeys and has been a success. In 1930, the total wild turkey population in the United States was estimated at 20,000 birds that lived in scattered, isolated areas in 21 states. Today, there are more than two million wild turkeys, found in every state except Alaska.

Trap-and-release programs have helped to reestablish many other wildlife species, such as beavers, trumpeter swans, whooping cranes, and wolves. Each time a population is reintroduced, this lessens the chance that the entire species can be wiped out by a disease or other hardship.

Zoos and Captive Breeding

Sometimes, a species dies out or is close to extinction for reasons other than lack of habitat. Sometimes the only hope of saving a species is to give it a chance in captivity, with the hope of later reestablishing the species in the wild.

Several species have been held in captivity for breeding, thereby preserving the species for later reintroduction into the wild. Species such as the American bison, red wolf, California condor, and black-footed

Where Zoos Get Their Animals

Historically, zoos contacted an animal breeder when they wanted a new animal. The dealer would then arrange for a field expedition to capture the animal. Zoos rarely do this anymore, for several reasons: Wildlife export has been restricted because of overhunting, poaching, and habitat loss. Sometimes a country with an indigenous species will give a rare animal to another country, such as when China gave two giant pandas to the United States. Most of the animals that zoos acquire are born in other zoos.

ferret are all examples of successful captive-breeding programs. The red wolf has been successfully returned to the wild in some locations. Habitat is often saved as a direct result of a captive-breeding and a reintroduction program when land is designated as a refuge to support newly released species.

Zoos provide an opportunity through their educational programs to make people aware of the different animal species that exist and their needs. Most zoos in the United States have made an effort over the years to save wildlife. Zoos and aquariums are popular places for people to visit. The educational programs they provide have been effective in making people aware of different animals and their need for survival. Some have even set up research centers and learned how to successfully breed wild animals in captivity. Today, zoos seldom have to take animals from the wild.

Zoo biologists also share information about their animals with other zoos. They even plan the breeding of their captive animals so that genetic diversity is maintained.

Wetland Management and Preservation

Other areas that are important to manage and preserve are wetlands. Wetlands are land areas that tend to be wet or are regularly flooded and have a water table that is at or above the surface for at least part of the year. Other names for wetlands are wet meadows, bogs, prairie potholes, bottomland hardwood forests, or freshwater marshes. Swamps are usually referred to as inland wetlands or lagoons, saltwater marshes, freshwater marshes, brackish and intermediate marshes, mangrove swamps, or coastal wetlands.

In any wetland, the relationships between plants and animals are very important. When human activities impact either plants or animals in wetlands, it inevitably affects the entire ecosystem.

The ecosystem of wetlands is very fragile—the impact of one small component can cause a destructive ripple effect. For example, wetlands provide homes for juvenile organisms that need the protection of the grasses, more shallow water, and a sufficient food supply to grow into adults. They also provide a temporary refuge for an extraordinary number of migrating birds. Wetland areas need to be protected so that they continue to function as protectors of coastal areas and wildlife.

Unfortunately, humans have impacted wetlands through the construction of canals. When water is diverted, wetland vegetation dies off, leaving many animals without protection and shelter. When the wetland ecosystem is severely impacted, wildlife becomes threatened, endangered, and sometimes extinct.

Wilderness Area Designations

A major benefit for the welfare of wildlife and ecosystems is the designation of wilderness areas. Two hundred years ago, before roads, trains, telegraphs, farms, ranches, and mining camps, most of the western United States was wilderness. By 1964, the American people realized that soon there would be no more natural lands left in the country. The Wilderness Act was created to save the last of the remaining wild lands from development.

President Lyndon B. Johnson signed the Wilderness Act on September 3, 1964. It established the National Wilderness Preservation System to "... secure for the American people of present and future generations the benefits of an enduring resource of wilderness...."

The wilderness areas that have been created by the federal government not only protect the biological diversity, but they preserve the beauty and historical perspective of the land. The wilderness program is an effort to preserve the land and its natural integrity. According to the Bureau of Land Management—a branch of the government in the Department of the Interior—wilderness areas are undeveloped land that is meant to retain its primeval character. It is protected and managed in order to preserve its natural condition. These lands contain features of scientific, educational, scenic, and historical value.

Wilderness areas are different from other areas of public land, such as national forests and national parks. Motor vehicles cannot be taken into wilderness areas so that the natural processes and peace of the land are not disturbed (with the exception of vehicle use needed for emergencies involving the health and safety of persons). Even though visitors cannot drive through designated wilderness areas, there are many recreational activities that are permitted, such as fishing, hiking, horseback riding, backpacking, camping, nature study, photography, and rock climbing. These are areas where people can go to experience the full effects of nature without human interference. Wilderness areas also provide the peace and solace animals need in order to function and survive in their native environments.

Although most of the designated wilderness lands exist in the western portion of the United States, there are also several designated areas in the East. Protecting wilderness keeps critical habitat areas from being developed and exploited for their natural resources. The time to act to conserve these resources for future generations to enjoy is now—because once these resources are gone, they are gone forever.

CONCLUSION: FUTURE ISSUES AND TRENDS

Species are an integral part of whole, interacting ecosystems. Ecosystems provide habitat for species and are essential for climate control and nutrient cycling. These whole systems must be conserved, protected, and preserved.

This book has illustrated what a critical resource animal species are, their uses and contributions to people's lives, the goods and services they provide, and how we must manage this precious resource so it will exist for future generations to enjoy. This chapter looks at the future of animals, the concept of backyard conservation, and how everyone can get involved.

THE FUTURE OF ANIMALS

When the pace of change is slow in an ecosystem, species can often adapt in order to survive. Those that cannot adapt become extinct. There have always been new species evolving to take their place. Today, however, extinction is happening more rapidly than the birth of new species. Unfortunately, humans are largely to blame. The world's rapidly growing population destroys more and more resources. As forests are cut down, land is cultivated, and areas are mined for minerals. Habitat is taken from animals, causing species to become threatened, endangered, and even extinct.

If this trend continues, it is not difficult to see where it will lead. Wildlife all over the world is struggling to survive—in faraway countries such as Africa, Asia, or Russia—as well as in our own backyards. All animal species require wild areas in order to thrive. It is important for us to save as much space for wildlife as we can. Humans need to remember that their actions today may affect the future survival of animals that are not yet endangered. It takes communities—even countries—working together to ensure the future of animals.

BACKYARD CONSERVATION

People can take action to help animals by starting in their own backyards. Many people set out bird feeders and birdbaths to help migrating and seasonal visitors. For people who live in remote areas that were once—or still are—part of wildlife habitat, landscaping with natural vegetation that local wildlife prefers can help during the long, cold winter months when food is scarce for many species.

Conservation also applies to communities. Species do not have to die out. Steps can be taken to protect them and ensure biodiversity for the future. The most important and obvious steps to take are to stop the continued destruction of their habitats and to try to repair as much as possible the damage already done. Endeavors, such as reforesting, may be necessary to protect and preserve species.

People are becoming more environmentally oriented, as the following statistics from the U.S. Fish and Wildlife Service demonstrate:

- There are 46 million bird-watchers in the country.
- Wildlife watching expenditures total $38 million each year.

Participating in backyard conservation efforts can provide an important assistance in supporting wildlife. (a) This yard in Iowa has birdfeeders and native prairie plants to provide food for passing animals. (b) Hummingbirds are frequent visitors in urban areas. Hanging out a hummingbird feeder helps these tiny birds. (*Courtesy of Natural Resources Conservation Service, by Lynn Betts*)

- The largest group of active wildlife watchers is in the age range from 35 to 44 years old (23%), followed by people 45 to 54 years old (22%).
- More than 66 million Americans spend some amount of time observing, photographing, or feeding wildlife.

WAYS TO GET INVOLVED

There are many ways to get involved and help in the conservation and preservation of animal species. One way to help stop species extinction is to not purchase products made from endangered species.

Learning more about animal species and their habitats is also important. Awareness and understanding promotes a more intelligent, informed use of resources. Remembering that many of our most precious resources are not renewable and conserving the Earth's resources for future generations—called sustainable use—can be critical for animals' as well as humans' survival. For example, the excessive use of automobiles and the continuation of industrial pollution contribute to the greenhouse effect. This can change the Earth's climate, which can then change other properties such as sea level, vegetation distribution, and the quality of the air. These things impact all life-forms.

A simple, but effective, way to become involved and help endangered species to survive is by joining clubs or organizations that aim to protect and conserve nature and wildlife. There are many organizations that work to support the habitat of animals. Some are general, and some are species-specific. Information about some of the various organizations is listed in the appendix.

It is important to remember that life is a complex system—involving millions of plants and animals working together. If one piece of this complex system is impacted, the natural balance and harmony of the whole system is upset. Humans may believe they fill the most important place in this system—but in reality, humans are but one small part working in the system with the rest of the life-forms.

Ultimately, keeping the system healthy requires everyone's efforts. Each one of us has something to contribute, just as each one of us can help protect and preserve animal species. By working together, we can keep other animals from experiencing the fate of the passenger pigeon, the dodo, and the California grizzly bear.

GLOSSARY

abiotic The nonliving components of a system, such as air, water, rocks, and energy.

aboreal Able to live in trees, like a parrot or an iguana.

antlers Growths on the head of a deer that shed every year and are made of bonelike material.

bachelor herd A group of nonbreeding males of the same species that forms its own herd away from the main herd that contains the females.

biodiversity The variety of different species of plants and animals found in an environment.

biologist A scientist who studies plant and animal life as well as natural life processes.

biology The science of studying natural life processes and plant and animal life.

biome A major ecological community type.

biostratigraphy The identification of fossils found within sedimentary rock strata as a method of determining the relative geologic age of the rock.

biotic The living components of a system, such as animals, plants, and microorganisms.

blubber A thick layer of fat that whales, sea lions, polar bears, and other marine mammals have; blubber helps to keep the animal warm.

breed To pick specific animals to mate and have young in order to create an animal with a particular appearance or behavior.

canine teeth In mammals, the teeth next to the incisors that are used for holding prey and/or tearing meat.

claws The "fingernails" of an animal such as a bear or cat; claws help the animal to grab prey; in birds, they are called *talons*.

cold-blooded Having a body temperature that changes with the temperature of the animal's surroundings.

community   An interacting population of various kinds of species in a common location.

competition   An active demand by two or more organisms or kinds of organisms for some environmental resource that is in short supply.

conservation   Careful management and protection of a natural resource.

consumers   Organisms that obtain food by preying on other organisms or by eating particles of organic matter.

cooperation   An association of species for a common benefit.

DDT   A colorless, odorless water-insoluble insecticide; it is an aromatic organochlorine that tends to accumulate and persist in ecosystems and has toxic effects on many vertebrates; it is now banned in the United States.

decomposers   Organisms that return organic substances to the environment by feeding on and breaking down dead protoplasm.

den   The home or dwelling of an animal, usually in the ground, a tree hollow, or a cave.

domestic animal   An animal that is bred to get along with people, such as a dog or cat.

dominance/dominant   Having the most influence, usually in a herd, group, or pack of animals.

down   Soft feathers that provide insulation for birds.

echolocation   A means by which bats and certain other animals can find their way, find food, or avoid obstacles by emitting a series of sounds, often inaudible to humans, which echo back from an object and are received by the ear.

ecology   The branch of science that studies the interrelationship of living things and their environment.

ecosystem   An interdependent community of plants and animals and their environment.

embryo   An animal or plant in the early stages of its development, between fertilization and hatching or birth.

endangered   In danger of becoming extinct.

endotherm   A warm-blooded animal; an animal that maintains its body temperature at a relatively constant level regardless of the temperature of the environment.

exotic   Special or unusual.

extinct   No longer living.

food chain   A way of showing who eats whom in the animal and plant world.

gene   The material inside a cell that determines the traits that living things inherit from their parents.

genetic diversity   The variety of genetic traits available to provide inheritable characteristics for a species.

geologist   A scientist who studies the history, formation, and processes of the Earth.

geology   The study of the history, formation, and processes that shaped, and continue to shape, the Earth.

gestation   The period of time during which a female mammal carries young in her uterus.

global warming   An increase in the average temperature of the Earth's atmosphere and oceans over time; this increase can cause changes in the Earth's climate that can affect habitats and the plants and animals that live in them.

guard hairs   The longer, stiffer hairs that grow up through the shorter, usually woolly hairs of a mammal's coat.

habitat   Where an animal or plant normally lives and grows.

herd   A group of animals that travels and feeds together.

hibernate/hibernation   To sleep or be in a dormant state during the winter season; hibernation is caused by cold winter conditions.

homing instinct   The ability to find a home.

horns   Growths on the head of an antelope, cow, sheep, or goat that are never shed.

incubate   The process of keeping eggs warm in order to hatch them.

inherit   To receive genetic traits from a parent.

invertebrate   An animal that lacks a spinal column.

keratin   A protein that hair, nails, skin, and horns are made of.

mammal   A member of a group of animals that has a backbone and feeds its young with mother's milk.

mass extinction   Many species becoming extinct at one time.

metamorphosis   The process by which some young animals, especially insects, become adults.

migrate/migration   To move/the seasonal movement of animals from one place of residence to another.

niche   A place or activity where an animal is best suited.

nocturnal   Awake and active during the night and asleep during the day.

omnivore   An animal that eats all kinds of foods, both plants and animals.

paleoenvironment   An environment that existed on the Earth in ancient times.

paleontologist   A scientist who studies life from past geological periods from fossil remains.

paleontology   The study of life from past geological periods from fossil remains.

PCB (polychlorinated biphenyl)   These are any of the compounds that are produced by replacing hydrogen atoms in biphenyl with chlorine; they have various industrial applications and are toxic environmental pollutants that tend to accumulate in animal tissues.

physiology   A branch of biology that deals with the functions and activities of life or living matter, and of the physical and chemical phenomena involved.

poacher   A person who illegally kills or captures wild animals.

population   The total number of individuals occupying an area.

predator   An animal that hunts and kills other animals for its food.

prey   An animal that is hunted and killed for food.

producer   An organism, such as a green plant, that is a source of biomass that can be consumed by other organisms.

rabies   A disease that affects the nervous system of mammals; symptoms include abnormal behavior; it often causes paralysis and even death.

reptile   A member of a group of animals that live on land, lay eggs, and are cold-blooded, such as alligators, turtles, snakes, and lizards.

scavengers   An organism that typically feeds on dead animals or garbage.

sedimentary rock   Rock formed by, or from, deposits of sediment.

social   Refers to animals that live in groups of communities.

social skills   Skills animals learn that help them live successfully in groups.

species   A group of individuals that have many of the same characteristics and are different from all other animals in some important way.

survival   The continuation of life.

survive   The ability of an organism to continue living or existing in its environment.

symbiosis   A cooperative relationship between two organisms.

tame   To make a wild animal behave in a way that is beneficial to humans.

taxonomist   A scientist who studies taxonomy.

taxonomy   The science of the classification of organisms; common names of plants and animals can very widely, but their scientific (taxonomic) names are accepted worldwide.

territory   The defended part of an animal's home range; a territorial animal is one that defends its territory against intruders.

threatened species   A species in danger of becoming extinct.

vertebrae   Bones that make up the backbone (spinal column).

vertebrate   An animal that has a spinal column.

Bush, Mark B. *Ecology of a Changing Planet,* 3rd ed. Upper Saddle River, N.J.: Prentice Hall, 2003.

Dewey, Jennifer Owings. *Wildlife Rescue: The Work of Dr. Kathleen Ramsay.* Honesdale, Pa.: Boyds Mills Press Inc., 1994.

Ford, Barbara, and Stephen Ross. *Wildlife Rescue.* Niles, Ill.: Albert Whitman & Company, 1987.

Goodman, Billy. *A Kid's Guide to How to Save the Animals.* New York: Avon Books, 1991.

Goodman, Susan E. *Animal Rescue: The Best Job There Is.* New York: Simon & Schuster Books for Young Readers, 2000.

Hansen, Ann Larkin. *Uncommon Farm Animals.* Edina, Minn.: Abdo Publishing Company, 1998.

Herda, D.J. *Environmental America: The North Central States.* Brookfield, Conn.: The Millbrook Press, 1991.

———. *Environmental America: The Northeastern States.* Brookfield, Conn.: The Millbrook Press, 1991.

———. *Environmental America: The Northwestern States.* Brookfield, Conn.: The Millbrook Press, 1991.

———. *Environmental America: The South Central States.* Brookfield, Conn.: The Millbrook Press. 1991.

———. *Environmental America: The Southeastern States.* Brookfield, Conn.: The Millbrook Press, 1991.

———. *Environmental America: The Southwestern States.* Brookfield, Conn.: The Millbrook Press, 1991.

Hurwitz, Jane. *The World of Work: Choosing a Career in Animal Care.* New York: The Rosen Publishing Group Inc., 1997.

Irvine, Georgeanne. *Protecting Endangered Species at the San Diego Zoo.* New York: Simon & Schuster Books for Young Readers, 1990.

Knight, Bertram T. *Working at a Zoo.* Danbury, Conn.: Children's Press, 1998.

Kress, Stephen W. *Project Puffin: How We Brought Puffins Back to Egg Rock.* Gardiner, Maine: Tilbury House, 1997.

Lowery, Linda, and Marybeth Lorbiecki. *Earthwise at Play.* Minneapolis, Minn.: Carolrhoda Books Inc., 1993.

Maynard, Thane. *Endangered Animal Babies.* New York: Franklin Watts, 1993.

Nirgiotis, Nicholas, and Theodore Nirgiotis. *No More Dodos: How Zoos Help Endangered Wildlife.* Minneapolis, Minn.: Lerner Publications Company, 1996.

Paladino, Catherine. *Our Vanishing Farm Animals: Saving America's Rare Breeds.* New York: Little, Brown, and Company Inc., 1991.

Pringle, Laurence. *Saving Our Wildlife.* Hillside, N.J.: Enslow Publishers Inc., 1990.

Smith, Roland. *Sea Otter Rescue: The Aftermath of an Oil Spill.* New York: Cobblehill Books, 1990.

Swinburne, Stephen R. *In Good Hands: Behind the Scenes at a Center for Orphaned and Injured Birds.* San Francisco: Sierra Club, 1998.

Zeaman, John. *Exotic Pets: From Alligators to Zebra Fish.* Danbury, Conn.: Franklin Watts, 1999.

WEB SITES

African Wildlife Foundation
http://www.awf.org
Works with the people of Africa to protect their natural resources.

Alliance for the Wild Rockies
http://www.wildrockiesalliance.org
Formed to meet the challenge of saving the northern Rockies bioregion from habitat destruction.

American Pheasant and Waterfowl Society
http://www.apws.org
Promotes the rights and interest of the members to keep and rear pheasants, waterfowl, and other upland aquatic and ornamental birds.

Appalachian Mountain Club
http://www.outdoors.org
Founded in 1876, it is America's oldest conservation and recreation organization. It is devoted to the protection and enjoyment of the mountains, rivers, and trails of the Northeast.

Bat Conservation International
http://www.batcon.org
Working to protect and restore bats and their habitats worldwide.

Caesar Kleberg Wildlife Research Institute
http://ckwri.tamuk.edu/
Providing science-based information for enhancing the conservation and management of wildlife.

California Waterfowl Association
http://www.calwaterfowl.org
Nonprofit conservation organization supporting waterfowl conservation, wetlands, and outdoor heritage.

Desert Tortoise Council
http://www.deserttortoise.org
Promotes conservation of the desert tortoise in the deserts of the southwestern United States and Mexico.

Ducks Unlimited
http://www.ducks.org.
Concerned with the annual life cycle needs of North American waterfowl by protecting, enhancing, restoring, and managing important wetlands and associated uplands.

Florida Panther Society
http://www.panthersociety.org
A nonprofit environmental education and support organization for the Florida panther.

Foundation for North American Wild Sheep
http://www.fnaws.org
Promotes enhanced and increased populations of indigenous wild sheep on the North American continent.

Great Bear Foundation
http://www.greatbear.org
Established to promote conservation of wild bears and their natural habitat worldwide.

Hawk Mountain Sanctuary Association
http://www.hawkmountain.org
Fosters the conservation of birds of prey and other wildlife to create a better understanding of the environment.

Inland Northwest Wildlife Council

http://www.wildlifecouncil.com
Nonprofit wildlife and conservation organization of the Pacific Northwest.

International Association of Fish and Wildlife Agencies

http://www.iafwa.org
An organization of public agencies charged with the protection and management of North America's fish and wildlife resources.

International Crane Foundation

http://www.savingcranes.org
Conservation of migratory cranes and their habitats.

International Primate Protection League

http://www.ippl.org
Working for the well being of primates.

International Rhinos Foundation

http://www.rhinos-irf.org
A corporation of institutions and individuals worldwide whose sole purpose is dedicated to the conservation of black, white, Sumatran, Javan, and Indian rhinos.

International Snow Leopard Trust

http://www.snowleopard.org
Dedicated to the conservation of the endangered snow leopard and its mountain ecosystem through a balanced approach that considers the needs of the people and the environments.

International Wolf Center

http://www.wolf.org.
Supports the survival of the wolf around the world by teaching about its life, its association with other species, and its dynamic relationship to humans.

Mountain Lion Foundation

http://www.mountainlion.org
Dedicated to the preservation and conservation of mountain lions and their habitat.

National Fish and Wildlife Foundation

http://www.nfwf.org
A nonprofit organization dedicated to promoting improved conservation and sustainable use of our nation's natural resources. Its goals are conservation education, natural resource management, habitat protection, ecosystem restoration, and public policy development.

National Wildlife Federation

http://www.nwf.org
Focuses its efforts on endangered habitat, water quality, land stewardship, and wetlands.

Natural Resources Conservation Service

http://www.nrcs.usda.gov

Developing and transferring practical social sciences technology to assist in the productive, equitable, and environmentally sound use of our natural resources.

Peregrine Fund

http://www.peregrinefund.org

Working to conserve wild populations of birds of prey.

RARE Center for Tropical Bird Conservation

http://www.fws.gov

Working to protect wild lands of globally significant biological diversity by empowering local people to benefit from their preservation.

Sea Turtle Preservation Society

http://www.seaturtlespacecoast.org

A not-for-profit organization whose members are permitted by the Florida Fish & Wildlife Conservation Commission and the U.S. Fish and Wildlife Service to work with endangered and threatened marine turtles.

Teaming With Wildlife

http://www.teaming.com

Geared toward conservation of America's wildlife and wild places.

Whooping Crane Conservation Association

http://www.whoopingcrane.com

A nonprofit organization working to advance conservation, protection, and propagation of the whooping crane population worldwide.

The Wildlife Conservation Society

http://www.wcs.org

An organization geared toward saving wildlife and wild lands throughout the world.

Wildlife Information Center

http://www.wildlifeinfo.org

Protecting wildlife and habitat through education, research, and conservation for the well-being of the Earth and all its inhabitants.

Wilderness Society

http://www.wilderness.org

Works to protect America's wilderness and to develop a nationwide network of wild lands through public education, scientific analysis, and advocacy.

World Wildlife Fund

http://www.worldwildlife.org

Dedicated to saving animal species worldwide.

JULIE KERR CASPER holds B.S., M.S., and Ph.D. degrees in earth science with an emphasis on natural resource conservation. She has worked for the United States Bureau of Land Management (BLM) for nearly 30 years and is primarily focused on practical issues concerning the promotion of a healthier, better-managed environment for both the short- and long-term. She has also had extensive experience teaching middle school and high school students over the past 20 years. She has taught classes, instructed workshops, given presentations, and led field trips and science application exercises. She is the author of several award-winning novels, articles, and stories.